LIVING TOGETHER

Your emotions
your finances
and the law

Libby Husemeyer

with the

Women's Legal Status Committee

SOUTHERN
BOOK PUBLISHERS

ISBN 1 86812 390 1

First edition, first impression 1991

Published by
Southern Book Publishers (Pty) Ltd
P.O. Box 3103, Halfway House, 1685

Cover design by William Steyn
Set in Bembo Roman 11 on 13 pt
by Book Productions, Pretoria
Printed and bound by Sigma Press, Pretoria

Preface

For many years, people involved in live-in relationships have contacted the Women's Legal Status Committee with questions relating to finances, property, housing, parenthood and custody. As a consequence, WLSC initiated an investigation into these aspects of live-in relationships and in November 1989 held a public seminar on cohabitation.

The next step is this book, which deals in depth with legal and emotional problems of unmarried couples living together and gives some practical solutions to situations that may arise.

WLSC has been in existence since 1975 and has researched legislation relating to marriage, divorce, the status of children, maintenance, employment and labour law and taxation, as well as abortion, rape and violence against women. The organisation lobbies government, commissions and other authorities and submits recommendations, many of which have subsequently been included in legislation.

Women's Legal Status Committee
June 1991

Acknowledgements

I had a lot of help from a lot of people in researching and writing this book. My grateful thanks go firstly to all the people who gave me permission to write about their personal experiences. Since most of them asked to remain anonymous, I have used pseudonyms throughout and I regret that I cannot thank them by name. Their stories bring the law to life, and the book would have been a very dry recital of facts without them.

I am especially indebted to my friend Gary Moore of Tonkin, Clacey, Anderson and Moore, who read the first draft with meticulous care. His comments were incisive and invaluable, and the book has benefited not only from his vast legal knowledge but also from his excellent editing.

I am also extremely grateful to Professor Paul Boberg for writing the Foreword.

Ruth Ward, Karen Shears, Lesley Kahn and other staff members of Wits Law Library were unfailingly pleasant and helpful.

Professor J C Bekker of Vista University, Philippa Kruger of Wits Law Clinic and Susan Bedil of Midrand Campus sent me useful material on legal aspects of living together, for which I am grateful. Thanks also to Mike Clacey, Charles Thatcher, Antoinette Ries of the Single Parents' Group and to my friend Wilna Botha for their help.

One of the things I enjoyed most about writing this book

was the regular contact I had with Roberta Johnston, Babette Kabak, Doris Ravenhill and Fran Cleaton-Jones of the Women's Legal Status Committee. They were extremely supportive and helpful, and though I am not sorry the book is finished, I shall miss our meetings!

Finally, I thank my husband Clint, who made me endless cups of tea and supported me in this project from start to finish, and my children Nicola, Victoria and Peter, who sacrificed a holiday without too many complaints when my deadline loomed!

Foreword

Human beings are naturally gregarious. They also have strong sexual instincts. And they experience a variety of emotions, the most basic of which are love, hate, greed and jealousy.

So it is understandable that they should look lovingly upon the object of their sexual desires, and want to share home and hearth with that person – in other words, to live together. Unfortunately, the tendency of humans to view a desired object with rose-coloured spectacles, investing it with all sorts of virtues bearing no relationship to reality and blithely ignoring its manifest vices, takes over here. As everyone knows, people in love are the worst possible candidates for a lecture on caution or an examination in common sense.

The three great events of human existence – birth, marriage and death – have long been regarded as the province of the church and the law. Every society prescribes a ceremonial manner of dealing with these events, and attaches a multitude of social and legal consequences to them. With primitive people these consequences are generally inescapable and immutable, and the price of disobedience is harsh. More sophisticated cultures tend to allow a limited choice of ceremonies and sequelae, and to tolerate a degree of dissidence. Until quite recently, however, our society still required a great deal of conformity from its members, especially in the field of sexual behaviour.

When it comes to marriage, modern men and women – so

the statistics and experience tell us – are increasingly resentful of these prescriptions of church and state. They shudder at the ceremonies so dear to the hearts of middle-aged matrons. They rebel against the social stereotypes and implicit sexism that they associate with the married state. They object to paying the higher income tax which our law imposed upon married couples until 1991. And – perhaps most significantly of all – if they have previously been divorced or are the children of divorced parents they associate the emotional trauma and the financial disaster of their past condition with the institution that began it all – marriage – and in some blindly unreasoning way hope to escape a repeat performance by eschewing the institution itself.

The truth, of course, is that the fault lies not with the institution but with those who embark upon it. It is not marriages, but people, who break up. Given the mixture of emotional involvement and human frailty that characterize most relationships, it is more remarkable when they endure than when they fail. The unhappiness that attends the ending of a conjugal relationship flows from the deprivation of consortium and cohabitation, not the dissolution of the legal marriage tie.

The heartbreak of losing a loved one – whether through death or mere human fickleness – is unavoidable. That the relationship was called a marriage will not diminish the distress. Not so, however, the financial implications. Here the couple who sought the blessing of church and state for their union have all the advantages.

The law regards the institution of marriage as the foundation of family life and hence of the state itself. And the law looks after its own. Therefore it has developed a multitude of rules for untangling the economic confusion that is often associated with the end of a marriage. Unless the parties have chosen to be married with complete separation of goods, the material prosperity to which both have contributed is shared. Maintenance and inheritance rights are recognized. If the union has brought forth children, the love of both parents for their progeny is respected and allowed expression as far as practical considerations and the best interests of the children allow.

The couple who cohabited without benefit of matrimony, on the other hand, may well find the dissolution of their relationship attended by more than mere misery. A financial debacle could await the partner whose contribution to the common home took the form of buying consumables or paying running expenses, leaving the other free to spend his income on more enduring assets.

Eviction from a house or flat bought with both incomes but registered in the name of only one partner could be the next blow. And, if there are children, the father who loved their mother too well to see any need for marrying her to confirm what they both already knew might find himself without any legal rights – even a right of access – to those children.

For our law, while tolerating cohabitation outside marriage, does nothing positive to help those who indulge in it. It takes the view that a couple who have disdained its institutions must suffer the consequences. While reform may come in the future, our present law has not, it seems, quite rid itself of the notion of 'living in sin'.

But those who reject marriage need not despair. Economic disaster is not the inevitable penalty for cohabition without matrimony. While the law offers no ready-made solutions of automatic application when unmarried couples part company, it does provide several methods of safeguarding the parties' interests when the relationship ends. Generally, those measures depend on the agreement or conduct of the parties *before* the end comes. Advance planning is the key concept.

That is where this book can help you if you plan to live with someone or are already doing so. It explains the legal position in simple yet accurate language, and gives sound, practical advice on how best to avoid most of the pitfalls. It will not help you avoid the heartbreak if your relationship ends. But then, neither will marriage. It will, however, help you avoid financial ruin. That is, if you read it and follow its advice. I recommend that you do so.

Professor P Q R Boberg
School of Law
University of the Witwatersrand

Contents

1

Introduction

If you are involved in a live-in relationship, you may not realise it but you are part of a social revolution. Thirty years ago almost no one lived together outside marriage. Today, throughout Western Europe and most of the English-speaking world, so many unmarried couples are living together that our concept of the family is changing fundamentally.

Since 1978, for example, the number of people living together in America has doubled every five years. In England living together is now so common, and the divorce rate so high, that researchers at the Family Policy Studies Centre believe the traditional family will soon become 'just a memory' for millions. They predict that by the year 2000 half the children in England will be growing up in single-parent homes or in homes headed by unmarried couples. Already more than a quarter of English babies are born outside marriage. In Sweden last year more children were born outside marriage than to married mothers. Over the last two decades the number of marriages in Denmark has declined by 42%, and 17% of all couples now live together.

The figures for South Africa are nowhere near as high – yet. (In the 1985 Census 3% of the total population classified themselves as 'living together'.) But the trend here is the same, and it is likely that where Britain is today we will be in ten to twenty years' time.

The change in attitudes has been equally dramatic. In the

1950s people referred to living together as 'living in sin'. They believed without questioning that if you loved someone you got married because, in the words of a song that was popular then, 'love and marriage go together like a horse and carriage – you can't have one without the other.' Anything else was scandalous and immoral.

Today, we don't use the phrase 'living in sin' any more: we talk about 'live-in relationships' or 'unmarried partnerships'. A young woman can tell her friends and co-workers that she is moving in with her boyfriend and chances are not a single eyebrow will be raised. Articles on living together have become a regular feature in mass-circulation women's magazines. The disapproval of the past has by no means disappeared completely; the Asian community is still strongly opposed, as are many people on the platteland and amongst the older generation. But society's attitude in general is increasingly tolerant and accepting. Living together is viewed by more and more people today as a respectable 'alternative lifestyle'.

Together, these changes have led many countries to grant legal recognition to the live-in relationship. In South Australia, for instance, a live-in relationship that has lasted five years or that has resulted in the birth of a child may be declared a 'putative' (reputed) marriage, with all the consequences of a legal marriage.

But this has not happened in South Africa. No matter how long you and your partner live together, your relationship is not recognised by the law. You have no legal obligations to one another, and the law will not protect you if your partner dies* or your relationship breaks up.

While your relationship may look exactly like a marriage – you may live together for years, have children together, buy a house together, do all the things a married couple does – none of the laws that safeguard the interests of a husband and wife apply in your case. In the eyes of the law you are simply two

---

* With one exception: see Workman's Compensation, Chapter 8.

single individuals who happen to have the same address.

This is of little concern if you are both students, with few assets and a combined income that doesn't stretch beyond the necessities. But it matters a great deal if you are working and accumulating assets or having children together. For example:

○ If your partner of many years dies without leaving a will, you will not inherit any part of his or her estate.
○ If you are injured or become seriously ill, your partner is not obliged to support you.
○ If you pay all the day-to-day living expenses and your partner buys the furniture, all the furniture will belong to your partner if you break up, and your partner will be under no legal obligation to reimburse you for what you have spent.

People do die, and most live-in relationships, unfortunately, don't last. It is neither morbid nor mercenary to consider those possibilities and take steps to protect yourself in the event that one or the other should occur – it is plain common sense.

This book looks at the emotional, legal and financial implications of living together. It offers no easy ways to protect yourself from the emotional risks of your relationship – unfortunately there are no easy ways. But it does suggest a number of ways in which you can protect yourself financially. The law may not provide you with a financial safety net; you can, however, provide one for yourself.

2

Why people live together

Living together means many different things to different people. For some it is just a temporary arrangement; for others it is a long-term commitment that resembles marriage in all but the legal details. Some choose a live-in relationship for financial reasons, some for companionship, others because they're head over heels in love ... or lust!

Some live together because they can't marry, some because they don't want to marry, some because they're scared of marriage, some because they think marriage is irrelevant. Still others see their relationship as a trial marriage.

And while for some people the decision to live together is a big step, to be taken only after careful deliberation, many others either leap impulsively or just drift into live-in relationships without thinking much, if at all, about their reasons for doing so.

However, virtually everyone who is living together today has been influenced in this choice by society's more tolerant attitude and by the fact that so many other people are doing it. Thirty years ago it was almost impossible even to think about 'living in sin'. Since then, 'the pill', the feminist movement, the student revolutions of the 1960s, urbanisation, increased mobility, the weakening of family ties and the declining influence of the church have all played a part in changing the way we think and behave. It is easy now, in an age that accepts a variety of alternative lifestyles, to opt for a live-in relationship.

For most people, in the end, the decision to live together is not prompted by any single consideration but by a mixture of often interrelated motives.

THE EFFECT OF DIVORCE

Twenty-five percent of divorced women in Britain are living with men outside marriage, compared to 10% of single women. In South Africa too, for both emotional and financial reasons, divorce has had a major impact on the number of live-in relationships.

Marie, a 32-year-old copy editor, divorced her husband five years ago after she discovered that he was having an affair. She has been living for the past two years with a journalist. 'Stefan and I love each other and he's much easier to live with than my husband was,' she says. 'He wants me to marry him, and if I hadn't been married before I probably would have said yes. But I'm terrified of making a second mistake and having to go through another divorce. People talk about the 'trauma of divorce' so much that it sounds trite, but it really was a very painful experience for me.'

She hesitates and then adds, 'It may sound irrational and superstitious – I suppose it is – but everything is fine between us now and I'm convinced that marriage would change that.'

Marie's fear of a second – or in some cases third or fourth – failed marriage is cited by many people as their reason for choosing to live with subsequent partners. And her belief that marriage would be the kiss of death for a successful relationship is shared by a surprising number of them.

The financial cost of divorce leads many men to choose a live-in relationship over a second marriage.

'I simply couldn't afford another divorce,' says Bob. 'My ex-wife and I agreed that she shouldn't go out to work until our youngest is in school full-time. That's another three years, so I'll be paying her maintenance for at least that long ... and of course child maintenance for another twenty years. I also let her have the house because I wanted the children to be affected as little as possible. Be-

5

lieve me, it's not easy to start all over again at the age of 36 with no house and half the income. But if I got married again and that marriage also failed, I could find myself paying alimony twice over, and then I'd be years older and even poorer. I'm not prepared to go any further backward.'

Bob is now living in a modest little house which he and his live-in partner Jennifer have bought together. Jennifer, a graphic artist, knew from the start that marriage was out. 'It doesn't worry me at all,' she says. 'I can understand why he's concerned about his financial security. Maybe I understand it more than most because I'm self-employed. Anyway, we're not starry-eyed teenagers. We care for each other but we're also practical. Neither of us could have bought this house on our own.'

The other side of the coin is that many women who are divorced from their husbands live with second partners instead of remarrying because the terms of their maintenance agreement stipulate that if they remarry, maintenance will cease.

It seems that the children of divorced parents are also more likely than those from stable homes to opt for live-in relationships in later life. Their home experience has made them wary of marriage: 'I never want to subject my own children to what I went through' is a typical comment. And while most don't rule out the possibility that they will marry one day, they want to make very certain that when they do, it will be to the right person. Many of them believe living together is the best way to do that.

TRIAL MARRIAGE

It is becoming increasingly common, especially among people in their twenties, to live together as a kind of test run for marriage. In a recent survey conducted by the English magazine *She,* an astonishing 93% of the 3 000 women who answered the questionnaire (mainly middle-class women aged 25 to 44) had lived with their husbands before they were married.

Leanne, a 24-year-old Durban travel agent, moved in with her boyfriend a year ago. 'I wouldn't even consider marrying someone

I hadn't lived with,' she says emphatically. 'My friends feel the same way. You learn more about a person by living with them for six months than you would in six years of dating every Friday night.'

She and her partner were seriously contemplating marriage, but now Leanne is concerned about his excessive drinking habit and has threatened to end their relationship unless he seeks help. 'Before, when we were just going out on weekends with a crowd of friends and he drank a lot, I told myself he was only letting off steam – you know, boys will be boys. It's because I'm living with him and see him coming home night after night and heading straight for the scotch that I know he has a serious problem.' She says that while it will be emotionally wrenching to leave him, she would find it far more traumatic to walk out if they were married.

Many trial marriages do end in marriage, however.

Angela and Bruce married last October after a two-year period of living together which she requested. She explains, 'I needed that time to sort out my feelings for Bruce. My father left my mother when I was very young. Bruce is 13 years older than I am and I was afraid that subconsciously I was seeking a replacement for my father rather than a husband. But now I know I wasn't.'

THE HIGH COST OF LIVING

Two can live as cheaply as one, according to the old saying. Well, not really – but two living together can certainly live more cheaply than two living apart. This is an important consideration for a number of people who choose live-in relationships, especially students and, at the other end of the spectrum, old age pensioners.

Students generally tend to view living together as a convenient, practical – and temporary – arrangement that suits their present stage of life. Like many other young people, they often feel too emotionally immature and unsettled to contemplate a permanent relationship. A study conducted at Columbia University in the United States found that only 26% of the women and 19% of the men surveyed would marry the person they were living with.

For senior citizens whose pensions and savings have been eroded by inflation, sharing expenses with a live-in partner can mean the difference between comfort and bare survival. Some of them, in fact, are caught in a double bind – they can't afford to live on their own, but they also can't afford to get married. According to the rules of many pension schemes, widows lose the right to their deceased husbands' pensions if they remarry.

Pensioners aren't the only ones who find that marriage carries a high financial penalty. Women teachers and nurses, for example, automatically lose their housing subsidies when they marry and cease to be the 'sole breadwinner'. The same applies to many other women in government or quasi-government employment. And until separate taxation was introduced for husbands and wives in the March 1991 Budget, joint taxation was another major obstacle to marriage for many.

Helen and James, both in their mid-thirties, lived together to avoid both higher taxation and the loss of a bond subsidy. Helen has a managerial position in a quasi-government corporation and James has his own business. When they met in 1984, Helen had just bought a house for which she received a housing subsidy amounting to approximately half her monthly payments, a total of over R9 000 a year. Not only would they have forfeited this subsidy if they had married, they also would have had to pay thousands of rands more in tax every year because of their high incomes. They decided to live together instead – though they subsequently married because they wanted to have children.

Finally, a number of older people opt for a live-in relationship in preference to remarriage to ensure that their estates will go to their children when they die.

GREATER FREEDOM AND EQUALITY

Johan and Natalie have been living together for 21 years and have two teenage children. Highly articulate and intelligent, they have a strong, loving relationship that is clearly based on mutual trust and respect. Most people who know them on a purely social level assume they are married. But they have rejected marriage in favour of a live-in relationship because it gives them a greater feeling of personal independence. Johan says, 'We know our association is completely voluntary, and that is important to both of us.' He emphasises, however, that a voluntary association such as theirs must be 'subject to certain economic safeguards to make it more secure'.

Johan's belief that marriage is restrictive is shared by a number of people, though not always for the same reason. Many feminists and career-oriented women, for example, argue that marriage subjugates women by perpetuating sex stereotypes of the husband as dominant partner, the wife as his dependant. A live-in relationship, in their opinion, offers the only possibility of a true partnership of equals.

FOR SOME, MARRIAGE IS IMPOSSIBLE

In some cases, couples live together because they cannot marry. For example, one or both of them may be underage and unable to marry without their parents' consent, which may be withheld. Alternatively, one or both of them may still be married to someone else. Until the Mixed Marriages Act was repealed, there were also numerous mixed-race couples for whom marriage was impossible.

SOME CONSIDER MARRIAGE IRRELEVANT

More and more people today believe that marriage offers no advantages over a live-in relationship and is simply irrelevant and unnecessary. Many qualify this, however, by adding that they still see a role for marriage when children are involved. Overseas, as we've seen, even this role is being undermined as increasing numbers of couples choose unmarried parenthood.

Gary and Lynn have been living together for over eight years. Both are in their late thirties, both have demanding professional careers, and they do not intend to have children. Gary says, 'If we got married tomorrow we wouldn't feel any differently. It wouldn't change our lives one iota. I love Lynn and I want to spend the rest of my life with her. I hope she wants to spend the rest of her life with me. But if she didn't, marriage wouldn't stop her from leaving me and I wouldn't want her to stay for that reason anyway. Marriage is just a piece of paper. In the end, the only thing that counts is your commitment to each other.'

THE DESIRE FOR COMPANIONSHIP

People are social creatures. However much we may enjoy our own company, most of us also want and need to share our lives with someone else, to have the companionship and love of a 'significant other'. Loneliness can be a powerful motivating factor in the decision to live with someone. Until recently this was one of the reasons why tens of thousands of black men and women, separated from their families by influx control laws, entered into live-in relationships in the cities where they worked. The desire for companionship is also an important consideration for many older people who, having spent most of their adult lives as part of a couple, suddenly find themselves alone when their spouses die.

Julia is an attractive, well-groomed woman in her mid-sixties. Her husband died unexpectedly of a heart attack nine years ago and Julia was devastated. They had had an extremely close and happy marriage and had never spent a night apart in over thirty years. Her daughters, who both live overseas, wanted her to live with them, but she couldn't bring herself to leave South Africa. So she coped with her grief by throwing herself into volunteer teaching. She says, 'I was fine as long as I was busy. But the evenings and the weekends and the holidays – I can't describe the loneliness I felt. It was almost overwhelming. When I look back on those first years I don't know how I ever got through them.'

Three years after her husband's death she had a chance meeting with Arthur, one of his former colleagues. Arthur had recently lost his wife and was feeling as lonely as she was. They began to meet every Saturday for lunch. At first their relationship was based on past associations and shared grief, but gradually they discovered they had many interests in common and spent more and more time together. 'In the end,' she says, 'there just seemed no point in our both going home to a lonely, empty house each night.'

They talked about getting married; even though Julia would have lost her husband's pension, they could have managed financially.

However, neither of them thought it was prudent to forfeit a source of income. 'We're both fit and healthy and we could live another twenty years,' Julia point out. 'If inflation continues at the same rate we could bitterly regret giving up that money in a few years' time.' Finally, with many reservations, they decided to live together.

It has proved to be a happy decision for both of them. Julia says that though her daughters often tease her about 'living in sin', they are also pleased. 'They knew how lonely I was and they were concerned about my safety. It's a relief to them to know I'm not alone any more.'

AIDS: THE FUTURE

According to a recent report, the number of people testing positive for exposure to the HIV virus in South Africa is currently doubling every 6,4 months. Given this staggering rate of increase, fear of AIDS is certain to become a paramount consideration for single young sexually active adults in the near future. What impact is this likely to have on live-in relationships?

In American cities where AIDS is already rife, people who in pre-AIDS days would have remained unattached and 'played the field' are tending to settle into stable – and AIDS-free – live-in relationships. Moreover, those who are already living together are staying together longer.

3

Your emotional relationship

Do you remember the old pop song *Breaking up is hard to do?* Well, staying together isn't easy either. Conflicts and irritations are inevitable whenever two people with different tastes and habits live at close quarters. This is something we tend to forget when we are in the first passionate throes of a love affair. Consciously, of course, we all know perfectly well that couples live happily ever after only in fairy tales and the pages of Mills and Boon. Yet deep down we still cling to the romantic myth that if our love is 'true', we will never bicker or argue or feel estranged from one another like others but will always live in perfect harmony together.

Somewhere in the world there may be two people who have achieved that blissful state. For the rest of us, unfortunately, learning to live with our partners requires constant effort and hard work, no matter how much we may love each other. It also takes a lot of qualities that most of us have in short supply, such as patience, humour, sensitivity, a willingness to compromise and an ability to listen. Even if you and your partner possess these virtues in abundance, you may find in the end that the differences between you are just too great to sustain your relationship.

Almost half of all marriages in Western countries end in divorce, and it seems that an even greater proportion of live-in relationships don't last. While it is easier in practical terms to end a live-in relationship than to end a marriage, it often in-

12

volves the same degree of emotional trauma. This chapter looks at emotional problems that you and your partner may encounter, or that may already be causing friction between you. Some of these are problems that are experienced by all couples, whether married or unmarried. There are other conflicts, however, caused by differing attitudes towards commitment and marriage, that are unique to live-in relationships.

FIRST THE HONEYMOON ...

Most relationships go through a honeymoon period, and when you and your partner first move in together you will probably experience a few months of blissful happiness. You will think everything your partner does is endearing and lovable. Your partner will think everything you say is witty and interesting. You will want to do everything and go everywhere together. No cross words or exasperated sighs or sulks will disturb the perfect tranquillity of your home. You may feel like 'Two souls with but a single thought,/Two hearts that beat as one', as a nineteenth-century poet wrote.

It is a wonderful time of your life. Enjoy every minute of it, because sooner or later the honeymoon inevitably comes to an end. The signs are unmistakable. One day the indulgent smile with which you formerly surveyed the mess your partner leaves in the kitchen every morning is replaced by a snarl. Romantic candlelit dinners and long cosy chats over coffee become a thing of the past when your partner puts a hundred watt bulb in the diningroom lamp and takes to reading the paper at the table.

You argue about which restaurant to go to and which movie to see, then your partner complains about indigestion all through the film and you fight about the quality of the acting all the way home. You don't like each other's friends. Your partner hates the cottage furniture you bought for the lounge and suggests that you exchange it for a black leather and chrome suite. You want to spend your next holiday in the Kruger Park; your partner prefers the South Coast. You do your best work late at night; your partner likes to go to bed at

13

nine and get up at five – both of you complain that the other is disturbing your sleep and being inconsiderate. The tension builds up until one day you think to yourself despairingly: we don't love each other any more – where did it all go wrong?

... THEN THE WORK

The truth is that nothing has gone wrong. You could not have prevented this situation by acting any differently. It is inevitable. No two people ever have 'but a single thought' for long. In *The Road Less Travelled* (Arrow Books Ltd, London, 1990, p. 93) M. Scott Peck describes what happens when the honeymoon comes to an end:

> ... both of them ... begin to come to the sickening realisation that they are not one with the beloved, that the beloved has and will continue to have his or her own desires, tastes, prejudices and timing different from the other's. One by one, gradually or suddenly, the ego boundaries snap back into place; gradually or suddenly, they fall out of love. Once again they are two separate individuals. At this point they begin either to dissolve the ties of their relationship or to initiate the work of real loving.

Thousands of books have been written on the subject of 'the work of real loving'. Women's magazines are full of articles with titles like 'Ten ways to put the love back into your love life', 'Twelve tips for better communication with your partner' and 'How to keep your partner happy/interested/ faithful.' It is far too big a topic for this book. But if you are having problems with your relationship or are trying to sort out your feelings towards your partner, you may find Scott Peck's book of value.

If you and your partner have a problem that you cannot solve on your own, counselling may help you as it has helped many others. Psychologists registered with the South African Medical and Dental Council are listed in the Yellow Pages. Or your doctor or one of your friends may be able to recommend a therapist.

Alternatively, you can contact the Family Life Centre (Famsa), which has branches throughout the country. Famsa's main purpose since its establishment in 1938 has been to improve marriage and family life and to help couples who are experiencing relationship difficulties. You can choose individual or joint counselling or a combination of the two.

Famsa also offers a programme called *Prepare/Enrich* that helps couples to identify areas of strength and areas that require attention in their relationship. Both partners answer a series of questions and their responses are then processed to define strengths and weaknesses in approximately two dozen categories including communication, emotions, sex and spiritual issues. The programme includes two feedback sessions with a trained counsellor and the cost is reasonable. Many church ministers recommend that couples do the programme as a preparation for marriage.

DIFFERING EXPECTATIONS

Despite the relative ease and frequency of divorce today few people enter into marriage casually. When a man and a woman get married it is usually because both want and expect to spend the rest of their lives together. One may love the other more, or be more committed to making the marriage work; they may discover later that they are incompatible and their marriage may end in failure. Nonetheless, their expectations and intentions at the beginning of married life are generally the same.

Very often this is not the case when two people move in together. As we have seen in the previous chapter, people choose live-in relationships for many different reasons. It could well be that your partner's reasons – and therefore his or her expectations of the relationship – are very different from your own. If your partner, for example, views living with you as a convenient temporary arrangement while you see your relationship as a long-term commitment leading eventually to marriage, you are almost certainly going to end up getting hurt.

Unfortunately it is hard to see how this can be avoided. Talking to each other about your expectations might help, but on the other hand there is a good chance it won't help at all. The trouble is that people are not always open or honest about their intentions. Many men are terrified by discussions of this nature and will say whatever they believe their partners want to hear in order to avoid an emotional scene. Many women are equally terrified of scaring their men off with talk about commitment and will pretend to be indifferent about the long-term prospects of the relationship when that is far from being a truthful reflection of their feelings.

Even when a man states flatly that he is not interested in marriage or commitment, the woman often either ignores the warning or assumes that she can change his mind.

Glynis, a 28-year-old personnel manager in Johannesburg, lived with Alex for eighteen months. She admits that she had only herself to blame for the heartache she felt when he left. 'He never lied to me,' she says. 'He told me about all his previous girlfriends – dozens of them. He used to laugh and say that his motto in life was "so many women, so little time". He often said two years was the maximum he was prepared to spend on any woman. But I just refused to believe him. He came from a broken home and I convinced myself that he really wanted commitment but was afraid of it because of the trauma his parents' separation had caused. All I had to do was love him without qualification and then all the barriers he'd built round himself would fall away. My friends kept telling me I was crazy, that no one was ever going to tie him down because he didn't want to be tied down. They were right ... he was right. I was the only one who was wrong. He's living with another girl now and I suppose she's deluding herself just as I did.'

Of course, it is not always the woman who wants commitment while the man jealously guards his independence. It may be the other way round. The point is, in any live-in relationship there is a possibility that one partner will want more from the relationship than the other is prepared to give. This situation almost always causes resentment and pain, and many live-in relationships end unhappily because of it.

THE BIOLOGICAL CLOCK AND CHANGING EXPECTATIONS

Many career-oriented women are too busy in their twenties pursuing professional goals to devote much time and energy to a relationship. Often all they want is simple uncomplicated companionship, and for years they may be happy with a no-strings-attached live-in arrangement.

But for many of these women there comes a time – commonly after they have turned thirty – when they discover that they are no longer satisfied with their lives. They feel restless and discontented with their relationships, and strangely flat and unexcited about career achievements that a few years before would have thrilled them. It often comes as a shock to them to realise that they have begun to long for marriage and children.

When they were in their twenties, having a family was something they could always think about later ... if at all. Once they reach their thirties, however, they become acutely aware that half their childbearing years have already passed, and that their biological clock is rapidly ticking away the remaining years. Then the urge to settle down and have children before it is too late can become almost overpowering.

When the nesting urge overcomes a woman who is involved in a live-in relationship, she almost always begins pressuring her partner to marry her. If he is also ready for a permanent commitment, all is well. Unfortunately it often happens that he is unwilling or unable to offer her the security she desires, either because he just doesn't love her enough to marry her or because he doesn't want to commit himself emotionally to anyone. Between her desire for marriage and his resistance to commitment there is little or no room for compromise, and the result is an unhappy stalemate which ends with one or the other deciding to call it quits.

17

Judith and Jeff

For Judith, a 34-year-old attorney, the realisation that her goals had changed was as sudden as a phone call. Her best friend's husband phoned to tell her that her friend had just given birth and, she says, 'I just burst into tears. I cried the whole day as if the world had come to an end. That evening I went to the nursing home to deliver flowers and the most peculiar thing happened. The woman at Reception asked me who the flowers were for and I gave her my own name. It was only after she'd checked the patients' list and told me there was no one registered under that name that I realised what I'd done.

'All of a sudden everything I'd achieved in my career seemed unimportant. I had this overwhelming desire to be married and have a baby. I can't tell you what a shock it was to realise that. I'd never been interested in children before. I come from a big family and my sisters were all married and had children. When we had family get-togethers Jeff and I were always glad to leave the mess and the noise behind and go home to our quiet, clean home.

'But that day our house looked completely different to me – it looked empty and sterile. I'm normally a very methodical, rational person and this sudden dramatic change was completely out of character. I can only think that it had been building up in my subconscious for a long time without my being aware of it. Magazine articles always talk about women's biological clocks ticking, but in my case it was more like the ringing of an alarm clock.'

Jeff, Judith's live-in partner of four years, was overseas on business at the time. The day he came back she cooked a special dinner and proposed to him over coffee. 'He was so astonished that he was quite literally speechless,' she recalls with a laugh. 'He said nothing for so long that I began to panic. Finally he joked, "I leave you alone for a week and look what happens," and then said very formally, "I accept."

'I asked him later why he'd never asked me to marry him. He said he'd always thought we should get married when we started a family, but he believed I had the right to decide when that would be because having a baby would change my life so much more than *his. He'd kept silent about marriage because he knew I loved my work and he didn't want to put pressure on me.' Jeff and Judith are now happily married and have a one-year-old son.*

Marie and Frank

Marie is a stylish, strikingly beautiful woman of 31 who works in the public relations field. She was 24 when she moved in with Frank, a decorator with his own successful business. For the first few years they were very happy together. Marie was independent and ambitious and 'didn't need marriage'. But as time passed she began to feel increasingly insecure.

A major source of worry for her was the fact that the house belonged to Frank. 'I consider it my house, my home,' she said. 'I've never paid Frank rent, but over the years we've changed the decor and I paid a lot of those expenses. But sometimes I feel like a boarder there. Whenever we have an argument I get into a state because I'm the one who would have to leave, and where would I go? I'd have to knock on a friend's door.'

When Marie was interviewed during the sixth year of their relationship she was clearly struggling to come to terms with a lot of inner conflicts. 'I will know when the time is right for marriage,' she said at one point. A few minutes later she said, 'I am basically married. I consider myself Frank's wife.' Later again she admitted, 'Maybe I would feel more secure if there was the commitment.' Then she added wistfully: 'In the end I ask myself why don't we get married? I always said I wanted a baby at 30, but I am 30 now and we've never come to grips with it.' And finally: 'It's always been a joke with our friends that I'm so opposed to marriage. But in the end I'm old-fashioned. I don't want children out of marriage.'

One year later, Marie has decided to move out. She puts a brave face on it and insists that it is an amicable separation. Frank is helping her to decorate her new flat. He has been 'a changed man' since she told him she is leaving, she says, and her friends all ask her how she has the heart to go ahead with the move. But she has thought long and hard about her decision and says she knows that she is doing the right thing. Frank wants her to stay – but on his terms. For Marie those terms are no longer good enough.

'My mum was super when I told her I was moving in with David,' says Mandy. *'I was only 23 then and she honestly thought it was better for us to live together than to rush into marriage. My two cousins had married very young and they were both divorced within three years. She didn't want me to do that. She disapproves of divorce. To her, marriage is for life and her attitude was "rather be sure first than sorry afterwards".*

'My father wasn't happy about it but my mum talked him round. I'd been living in a flat on my own for a year and they'd been worried about my safety, so she just kept telling him how relieved she was that I would no longer be so vulnerable with David there. Dad and David were a bit strained with each other for a while but once they discovered that they're both cricket fanatics everything was fine.'

Four years later, Mandy and David are still living together. Surprisingly, it is now Mandy's relationship with her mother that is strained. *'It began about a year ago,'* says Mandy. *'She started telling me she and dad want to see me "settled". I told her I am settled, but she just pursed her lips and said I knew what she meant. Then she started going on about how it's all very well when you're young to live for the day, but there comes a time when you have to think about the future and where you're going and so on.*

'She would never actually come out and say in so many words that she thought it was time we got married and had a family, but of course that's what she was getting at in a roundabout way. I know how much she and dad would love a big wedding celebration, and I know my mum is dying to have grandchildren. I feel guilty sometimes that I'm robbing them of these things, especially since I'm an only child. But if David and I ever do get married and have children, it will be when it suits us, not when it suits my parents.

'The thing is that my mother's attitude is beginning to cause problems between David and me, even though we're on the same side, so to speak. We went to visit mum and dad one Sunday a few months ago and mum spent most of the afternoon talking about two of her friends from bowls who had just become grandmothers and

20

how beautiful the babies were. David was irritated and said to me on the way home that he wished she'd lay off or words to that effect. I'd also been irritated, but I was furious with David for saying that. I found myself defending my mother and attacking him. I said she only wanted what was best for me and she had every right to long for grandchildren and we couldn't expect her to have our ideas about marriage because she came from an older generation that believed in it ... I went on and on and by the time we got home we weren't speaking.

'I phoned my mum the next day and yelled at her for interfering. She was really hurt and the few times we've seen her since then she's been very cool and formal. David and I got over our fight but now there's an undercurrent of tension that was never there before. I keep thinking how ironic it would be if my mother's desire to see us married was the thing that ended up driving us apart.'

Mandy's story is not unique. It seems that many parents today who initially accept a son's or daughter's live-in relationship grow impatient and upset after a time when the couple shows no sign of setting a wedding date. Like Mandy's mother, they long to see their children 'settled' – and in parents' vocabularies that invariably means 'married'. Parental pressure may take a variety of forms, from more-or-less tactful hints or jocular asides to thinly veiled emotional blackmail or a sustained, overt campaign. Parents who begin with subtle prodding may become increasingly vocal over time, especially if the live-in couple announces that a baby is on the way. The end result is usually stress and friction all round.

Then, of course, there are still many parents who are strongly opposed to living together for religious or moral reasons. If their offspring become involved in a live-in relationship, they often try to conceal it from their parents. Such deception is extremely stressful and generally has a detrimental effect on their relationship.

LIVING TOGETHER AS TRIAL MARRIAGE: DOES IT WORK?

As mentioned in the previous chapter, many live-in couples –

perhaps even most – regard their relationship as a trial marriage. They believe that by living together they come to know each other far better than they could otherwise; this gives them a sound basis for judging whether they are truly compatible and ready to make a lifelong commitment to one another.

If living together really is a good barometer of compatibility and marriage readiness, then live-in couples who subsequently marry should have a higher marital success rate than others. No research has been done on this subject in South Africa. However, an American follow-up study of 102 couples in their fourth year of marriage who had previously lived together for more than two years indicated that their live-in relationship had had no discernible effect on marital adjustment. In another study that followed 739 individuals between the ages of 17 and 24 for a nine-year period, the divorce rate was actually *higher* amongst those who had lived together prior to marriage.

These studies are probably not representative enough to draw any firm conclusions; the sample group in the first study was small and the respondents in the second were very young. But it is significant that ministers of religion here agree with their results. For example, the Anglican Bishop of Johannesburg, Bishop Duncan Buchanan, says: 'Our experience is that people who live together and then marry have a higher incidence of divorce, often within the first eighteen months. Living together does not prepare them for marriage.'

Dominee P Mellet of the Dutch Reformed Church, Johannesburg North, concurs. 'One of the most crucial elements in a sound relationship is commitment, but in my experience that commitment is almost always absent when couples live together,' he says. 'The man likes to have a back door open in case something better turns up, and time and again the girl is left in the lurch. I counselled a 35-year-old woman recently who lived with a man for five years. He was full of promises, but then she conceived and he dropped her, just like that. In the majority of cases that I've encountered, when couples who live together get married the results are disastrous.'

Chief Rabbi CK Harris says that most of his rabbis discourage living together because 'it is a false relationship. It is based on selfish motives and not on lasting commitment to each other and to family life. We're also worried about the damage it does psychologically, especially to the woman, who is usually more sensitive and takes these things more to heart.'

Whether you agree with the above comments or not, they certainly raise some troubling questions about the validity of regarding living together as a good test for marriage. For all their superficial similarities, living together in the end is a no-strings-attached relationship, while marriage, above all, is about commitment. That doesn't mean that you and your partner will not make a success of it if you get married; it does seem to indicate, however, that living together beforehand will not make your adjustment to married life any easier.

THE TRAUMA OF BREAKING UP

Many people believe it is less traumatic emotionally when a live-in relationship ends than when a marriage fails. Gail, who has been through both, disagrees. The break-up of her seven-year relationship with Dieter left her so deeply depressed that she had a nervous breakdown. A year later she still cries easily and her voice trembles when she talks about it.

She met Dieter, a German engineer, when she was in her late thirties. She had just divorced her husband of 18 years and was working for a legal firm to support herself and her two children. Dieter had recently separated from his wife. Nine months after they met, Dieter moved into her rented flat. He was experiencing financial difficulties at the time; his contract in South Africa had expired and he was unemployed. In addition, his capital was tied up in Germany until his divorce could be finalised. So Gail paid all their living expenses – the rent, the groceries, the maid, the telephone and electricity accounts.

'It never worried me that I was paying for everything,' she says. 'Our feelings then were very strong. It was a lifelong commitment. My trust in men was very low after my divorce. He was trying to

build it up.' Dieter was soft-spoken and gentle, and kind to Gail's children. In many ways he was the antithesis of her former husband who, though a good provider, had had an uncontrollable temper.

After Dieter's divorce was settled he brought his money over from Germany. Gail continued to pay for rent and food. Dieter bought groceries from time to time but spent most of his money on a R40 000 sound system and expensive motorcars – a BMW, a kombi and a sportscar. He gave Gail the sportscar, but registered it in his name. When they needed furniture Dieter paid for it; Gail never had any money left over at the end of the month. Gradually they replaced a lot of her old things.

After they had been living in the flat for several years Dieter decided it was too small, so he found them a house and put the lease in his name. His parents came to visit and stayed for six months. His daughter lived with them for two years. Later his 20-year-old stepdaughter spent a year with them and paid R300 a month towards her keep, which Dieter pocketed. Meanwhile, Dieter had started his own business, which wasn't going well. He was perpetually short of money and his contribution to the household, small as it had been, dwindled still more.

Seven years passed. Then one night two weeks before Christmas, Dieter told Gail that his feelings had changed. His announcement came like a bolt out of the blue – he had given no indication of unhappiness whatsoever until that night. Gail was devastated. She said to him, 'If that's how you feel, one of us will have to move.' He replied, 'Well, the lease is in my name.' Then he opened his briefcase and produced a typed agreement all ready for her signature. The agreement stated that she could take out of their joint home what she had brought into it. 'I was in such a state I just signed it,' Gail says. 'But looking back, I think I also signed it out of a perverse sort of pride – I wanted to show him that I was strong, that I could cope with anything he threw my way.'

Gail and her two children moved out three days before Christmas. There was little to move – they had given away most of her old furniture and all the new furniture belonged to Dieter. Gail was still making excuses for his behaviour to her parents, telling them that he was under stress and needed time to himself,

24

when she learned that his new girlfriend had moved in the day after she had moved out. The girl was an acquaintance of Gail's whom she had entertained in their home. A few days later Gail saw her driving the sportscar: Dieter had demanded that Gail return the keys to the car when she left.

Gail was an emotional wreck, but she had to pull herself to-gether to cope with the disastrous financial situation she found herself in. Over the last few years she had lived with Dieter she had gone into debt just to cover day-to-day living expenses; now she owed R2 500 on her credit card, most of which had gone on groceries. She and her children needed a roof over their heads, and she had to have a car.

Her company gave her a loan to cover the first month's rent plus deposit on a flat, and a further loan of R2 000 which she used to buy an old second-hand Opel. In addition, the attorney for whom she worked drafted a letter of demand which she sent to Dieter. The following week Dieter came to see her, pleading financial difficul-ties, and persuaded her to tear up the letter.

Some months later Dieter begged her for a reconciliation. Things hadn't worked out with the new girlfriend and it had all been a terrible mistake. Gail took him back. He gave her the keys to the sportscar once again, sold her Opel ... and kept the money. (Gail has a legal claim against him for doing so, but she says she is too embarrassed to tell her employer about it.) Three months later Dieter moved out. Then Gail broke down completely. Because she was incapable of looking after her children, they went to live with their father. Gail now lives alone and sees her son and daughter every other weekend.

Gail's story is horrifying, but at the same time revealing, be-cause it provides a textbook example of what not to do in a live-in relationship. Firstly, the financial arrangement she had with Dieter was grossly unfair. Gail's employer calculated that her relationship had cost her between R30 000 and R40 000 over the seven-year period. Secondly, she had no security of tenure because the lease on the house was in Dieter's name. In evicting her he was exercising his legal right as sole tenant.

It was not inevitable that Gail would end up homeless and nearly destitute. These consequences flowed from decisions Gail made or acquiesced in during the course of the relationship. Both could have been avoided (see Chapters 5 and 6).

As serious as these consequences were, they were overshadowed by the emotional trauma that Gail went through. But here too, however hard and unfeeling it may sound to say so, Gail was partly responsible. To continue to trust someone who has demonstrated over and over again that he cannot be trusted is self-defeating, self-destructive behaviour. Gail realises that now. She says, 'I was a fool, a total fool. I made a martyr of myself. I trusted him completely, but I guess I was believing in a phantom.'

4

Your relationship and the law

'[A] man and a woman who live together outside marriage are not prosecuted under the law but they are not protected by it. They are outside the law. Their union is not recognised, no legal obligation is implicit in it and an express obligation will not be enforced by the law.' (Patrick Devlin, *The Enforcement of Morals*, 1965.) Devlin was writing about English law in the early 1960s but his description fits South African law today, with one exception: it is likely that our courts will now enforce express obligations between live-in partners (see Chapter 9).

What does this mean in practical terms? It means that your relationship, while it may have the *appearance* of a marriage, has none of the legal *substance* of a marriage. Marriage is a legally recognised institution; a live-in relationship is not. You and your partner are 'strangers in law', as an English judge once said. A husband and wife are required by law to support one another financially, to be faithful to each other, and to give each other company and support (consortium). Two people who live together have none of these obligations; they also have none of the rights that flow from them.

An unmarried woman whose partner leaves her is not entitled to maintenance. The courts will not intervene to ensure that property and assets are divided fairly when they part. If a woman's live-in partner is killed at the hands of a third party, she has no right to sue for damages. If he dies without leaving a will, she will inherit nothing (and vice versa).

Live-in partners are not entirely ignored by the law. The Aliens Act of 1937, for example, permits a woman who lives with a man as his 'putative wife' to assume his surname, or subsequently to revert to her prior name, without official authorisation. The Workmen's Compensation Act provides for payment of compensation to a man's live-in partner in some circumstances. Live-in partners also come in for some unwelcome attention in the Insolvency Act of 1936 – but that is about the extent of it.

COMMON-LAW MARRIAGE IS NOT RECOGNISED IN SOUTH AFRICA

Contrary to widespread popular belief there is no such thing in South African law as common-law marriage, even though the term is often used to describe live-in relationships. The term originated in England centuries ago at a time when the common law permitted a man and a woman to marry simply by declaring that they took each other as husband and wife. The marriage became binding when it was consummated. However, common-law marriage has not been legal in England since 1753.

It is still possible to contract a common-law marriage in certain parts of the United States. In Scotland, too, a marriage 'by cohabitation with habit and repute' may be registered. This is not the case in South Africa. No matter how many years you and your partner live together, your relationship is not recognised by the law except in the specific Acts mentioned above.

OUR LAW PROTECTS MARRIAGE AND THE FAMILY

Why is the law like this? Why are people who live together treated so differently from people who are married?

The reason is that our society, like any other, promotes and protects institutions which it believes are beneficial and strives to discourage those which it believes are not. One of the institutions it protects is the family, because it is the basic social unit of our whole society and, in general, provides the best environment for raising children and for the emotional and material well-being of adults.

Protecting the family means, at the same time, protecting marriage. This is because our law still reflects the traditional view that sexual intercourse belongs inside marriage and that extramarital sex is immoral and ought to be discouraged. The *Oxford English Dictionary* (1990) may define 'family' as 'a set of parents and children', but in South African family law a family consists of a set of *married* parents and children.

IS REFORM NEEDED?

A marriage-based definition of family worked well before the 1960s. Until then almost everyone got married and lived in nuclear families, and few would have disagreed that sex outside marriage was sinful. But is it still adequate today? Living arrangements and public attitudes have changed a great deal in the past thirty years. It is true that most people still marry, but more and more couples are living together and having children outside marriage, and many South Africans no longer regard such relationships as immoral.

The way in which we define family is important, because if the definition is broadened to include unmarried partners, then they should be eligible for at least some of the protections of family law. South African law-makers have not yet dealt with this issue as the number of people involved in live-in relationships is still relatively small. However, many Western countries have tried – or are trying – to redefine the family in a way that reflects present-day realities, and to reassess family law in light of the new definition. Unfortunately, their experience shows that this is no easy task.

The case against reform

Many respected legal experts believe there is no need for reform. They argue that the law must respect the freedom of the individual to make his or her own choices – even if they are bad choices. Also, they say, it is unreasonable for live-in partners to want the benefits of marriage when they have not paid the costs. Homer Clark Jr. wrote in an American law journal in 1975:

> Whatever the social reality may be, it may still be efficient and not inequitable to retain conventional marriage as the criterion for property rights and duties. Individuals who wish to undertake those rights and duties then have a clearly defined method for doing so. Those who do not wish to undertake them have an equally clearly defined method for avoiding them, that is, by not marrying. Those who advocate the freedom that accompanies the refusal to marry but who at the same time wish the law to impose property rights and duties upon cohabiting but unmarried people are indulging in the great American dream of wishing to have their cake and eat it too. This is a common natural desire, but not one that the law is equipped to fulfill. The meaning of freedom in this context is the absence of legal regulation. Its virtue is that it leaves with individuals the power to work out their own personal relationships. Its defect is that they alone are responsible when those relationships become painful.

The final report of the South Australian Royal Commission on Human Relationships came to much the same conclusion in 1977: 'If parties refrain from marrying because they do not want to incur the legal and financial obligations of marriage, then the law should be slow to impose those obligations on them.'

The case for reform

Existing law, critics argue, leaves naive, unsophisticated or overly-trusting individuals at the mercy of their more shrewd and calculating partners. In washing its hands of disputes between unmarried partners, the law is in effect sanctioning unjust and unfair behaviour.

Moreover, they point out, not all people who live together do so out of a desire to avoid marital obligations. Many have

30

very different reasons for choosing cohabitation over marriage, and some drift into live-in relationships without any particular motive at all. It is unfair to deny these people legal protection on the grounds that they want rights without obligations, because rejection of obligations was not a factor in their decision.

Allowing live-in partners to regulate their own relationships by means of a cohabitation contract is not a satisfactory solution either, they say. Contracts benefit mainly people who are middle-class, well-educated and self-assertive. Those who are less well educated tend not to use them. In any case, a contract may be unfair if, as often happens, the two partners have unequal bargaining power.

John Eekelaar, a lecturer in law at Oxford University, believes that the 'protective, adjustive and support functions' of family law should be applied to unmarried partnerships. This, he argues, 'is wholly consistent with the proper role of family law, for the family is a social as well as legal unit and the need for protection and assistance in adjustments exists whatever the formal legality of the relationships.' *(Family Law and Social Policy*, 1978).

Problems posed by reform

The law as it exists now at least has the advantage of being simple and straightforward: if you are married, you are protected by family law; if you aren't, you're not. But if it is decided that reform is necessary, law-makers are immediately faced with a host of questions to which there are no easy answers.

Firstly, should all live-in partners be subject to family law, or only some? It doesn't make sense to apply the law to couples whose relationships are temporary or short-lived. Should it, then, be left up to the courts to decide in each case whether a relationship has 'the appropriate degree of apparent permanence and stability' (in the words of an English Court of Appeal judge) to resemble marriage and therefore qualify for legal protection? This approach can obviously lead to great inconsistencies.

Alternatively, should some arbitrary standard be set? The Canadian province of Ontario, for example, requires that a relationship last at least five years or that it be 'a relationship of some permanence where a child has been born'. Another Canadian province, British Columbia, has chosen a much lower qualification of two years. Arbitrary standards such as these can cause hardship in borderline cases and may be abused by individuals who avoid legal consequences simply by leaving the relationship just before the required time period has elapsed.

Secondly, in countries like South Africa that have different property regimes for marriages, which should be applied to unmarried partners – the accrual system, community of property, or complete separation of property? Spouses choose the system they prefer at the time of their marriage. Unless unmarried partners do the same, or the law decrees arbitrarily that, say, the accrual system will be applied to all live-in relationships, there are bound to be disputes when relationships end and property and assets must be divided. One property regime will benefit one partner, another will benefit the other, and the court will be faced with an impossible decision.

Furthermore, from what date should these property regimes commence? In a marriage, obviously, they begin on the day the marriage takes place. But what should be the starting point in the case of a live-in relationship? The first night the couple sleeps together? The day they move in together? Or some later date when their relationship is judged to be well-established? And what should the court decide if the couple can't remember the date they moved in together, or if they disagree about it?

Finally, should all laws pertaining to married couples apply to live-in partners, or only marriage law, or only a part of marriage law? Should the marital duties of fidelity and consortium be imposed on them? Should an unmarried partner be regarded as a spouse for the purpose of inheritance if his or her partner dies without leaving a will?

A third option

Leaving live-in couples without any legal protection as is the case at present can result in great personal hardship. Extending to them all the protections of marriage law poses enormous problems and makes marriage — except in a religious sense meaningless. Between these two poles there is a third option which Britain, for example, has adopted. That is to leave marriage law for marriage, but to use other existing laws to redress injustice at the end of a live-in relationship.

British law is different from South African law and the law of constructive trust that British judges have used could not be used here. But perhaps in the coming years South African judges will interpret our laws concerning unjust enrichment and universal partnership (see Chapter 8) more flexibly in order to bring about more fair and just property settlements when unmarried partnerships break up.

LOVER BEWARE

In the meantime, the law is what it is. As John Adams said in 1770: 'Whatever may be our wishes, our inclinations, or the dictates of our passions, they cannot alter the state of facts ...' Whether or not you believe it is fair, the fact is that the law will not protect you if your relationship goes horribly wrong. If you feel strongly enough that the law is unjust, you could form a lobbying group to press for reform as TUFF has done (see Chapter 7). Until such time as the law is changed, however, the only rational course is to take steps to protect yourself.

This is not the only instance where the law does not protect us from the consequences of our actions. For example, we all know the maxim 'buyer beware'. It means that the buyer alone is responsible if dissatisfied. Most of us learn the wisdom of it the hard way when we buy shoddy merchandise and then discover that we cannot return it. Perhaps what we need is another maxim, 'lover beware', for live-in partners. Because the cost of failing to 'beware' in a live-in relationship can be a great deal higher than the money you waste on a toaster that won't pop up or a jersey that shrinks after the first wash. It can, in fact, be a very expensive lesson to learn the hard way.

THIS BOOK AND THE LAW

The aim of this book is to provide a general guideline to the legal issues that are frequently encountered by live-in partners, and to suggest ways in which some of the more common pitfalls may be avoided. But it is not a substitute for expert legal advice. The law is extremely complex because people and their relationships are complex. If you have a legal problem, you need professional counsel.

5

Rands and sense

'We met at a housewarming party when I was 24,' Linda recalls.
'I walked into this crowded room and Richard was the first person I
saw. He asked me to dance and we spent the rest of the evening
together, talking and talking, exchanging all the usual information
about each other. We had so much in common – we loved the same
movies, the same books, we even belonged to the same squash club.

'From that night we spent every possible minute together. More
and more of my clothes ended up at his flat, and one day about four
months later I realised I hadn't been to my own flat in over a week.
We talked about it that night and Richard suggested that I give up
my flat and move in. He said with the money we saved on rent we
could buy some decent furniture and pay for an overseas holiday. I
didn't have to be persuaded: I was crazy about him.

'At the end of the month Richard borrowed a bakkie and we
moved my things. It only took two trips. I didn't have much furniture – most of the space was taken up by clothes and books.

'I offered to pay half the rent on the flat, but Richard said he'd
always paid by stop-order and might as well continue. We never
discussed finances again. It didn't worry me at the time – in fact, I
was relieved. It just seemed so tacky to talk about money. He hated
shopping, so I bought all the groceries, and I also paid the telephone and electricity accounts. Richard paid for all our major
purchases – a new sound system, a lounge suite, a microwave ...
lots of things over the years.

'It seems ironic now, but I thought he was getting the bad end of the bargain, so every Friday I treated him to dinner at a good restaurant. My mother thought I was being extravagant and said I should be putting money aside for a rainy day. I just laughed and told her not to worry – if a rainy day ever came, Richard would look after me. For our first "anniversary" I paid for a holiday in the Seychelles. The following year I had to go to London on business and I bought an air ticket for Richard so that he could go with me.

'We lived in the flat for almost four years. Then Richard changed jobs, and his new company had a bond subsidy scheme for employees. One Sunday he suggested that we go and look at townhouses. He said he'd saved enough for a deposit, and with the subsidy he'd be able to meet the bond repayments. I was thrilled at the thought of having a place of our own, but at the same time I was disconcerted. I had no idea he'd saved so much money. He was very secretive about some things – in all the years we lived together, he never told me how much he earned.

'A few months later we found a townhouse we both liked. He told me casually, as he signed the offer, that according to the terms of the bond subsidy scheme the property had to be registered in his name. That really upset me: I'd taken it for granted that the house would belong to both of us. In the car on the way back to the flat I guess I was very quiet, because he asked me in an irritated voice what was wrong. I told him, trying to sound calm and unemotional, though I felt like crying. He just snapped back that he hadn't written the rules of the scheme.

'We moved in in December and I spent my entire bonus on paint and curtains and plants for the garden. Looking back, I don't know why I did that. Ever since he'd started his new job he'd been bad-tempered and irritable, but I stupidly put it down to the fact that he was under a lot of stress at work.

'Over the next year things became steadily worse. We bickered about everything, and Richard started coming home late every evening. Then one Friday night he didn't come home at all. I was in too much of a panic to sleep, and by the time he showed up the following morning I was nearly sick with worry. That's when he told me he'd been seeing someone else at the office for months and wanted me to move out.

'I was devastated. There I was, 29 years old, and all I could do was run home to Mummy. I had nowhere else to go. If my parents hadn't been living in the same city, I don't know what I would have done. The following day my two brothers and I took a bakkie to the townhouse to move out all my things. Richard was in the garden; I couldn't face talking to him, so my older brother went out to discuss with him how we should divide up the furniture. Richard replied that it all belonged to him and that he had the receipts to prove it – if we removed anything that he'd paid for, he would contact his lawyer.

'So in the end it only took two trips to move my belongings, just the same as when I moved in with him. That's all I had after five years. I'd spent every cent I earned, but the house, the furniture, everything was Richard's.

'For a week all I did was cry. Then one morning I woke up in a rage about the injustice of it all. So I went to see a lawyer and told him the whole story. But he just shook his head and explained that there was nothing he could do to help me because the law doesn't protect live-in lovers. They have to protect themselves, and I hadn't done that.'

FIRST THE BAD NEWS ...

Most live-in relationships don't end as badly as Linda's did. Most people don't behave as callously or as selfishly as Richard did. But some do. As unmarried partnerships become more and more common, the number of people (almost always women) who find themselves in the same situation as Linda when their relationships end is also increasing. However unfair it may seem, virtually nothing can be done about it afterwards.

If Linda had been married to Richard, she would have been legally entitled to half their joint estate upon divorce (if they had married in community of property), or to half of all the assets they acquired during their marriage (if they had chosen the accrual system). But she and Richard were not married.

37

Secondly, there is no such thing in South African law as a common-law marriage. Like many others, Linda was under the impression that couples who live together for two years (some say five) are deemed to have a common-law marriage, and that this gives them certain rights. This belief is so widespread that it is very hard to eradicate, but it is completely untrue. Unfortunately, it lulls many into a false sense of security from which they are rudely awakened only when it is too late.

But surely there are other laws to protect people like Linda? There is little cause for optimism here, either. It is true that there is a principle in Roman-Dutch law that no one should be unjustly enriched at another's expense. But there is no comprehensive law that can be applied whenever unjust enrichment takes place. A case for unjust enrichment can be made only if it meets certain strictly defined conditions, and it seems that disputes involving live-in partners do not normally do so.

However, there may be exceptions. The late Professor H.R. Hahlo wrote: 'Where a man and his mistress have pooled their means for the purchase of a house which was registered in the man's name, and it is clear that the mistress did not intend a donation, she may be entitled to a share in it or, at least, to repayment of her contribution on grounds of unjust enrichment.' The law of enrichment actions is extremely complicated and the only way to determine whether an action for unjust enrichment exists in a specific case is to consult a lawyer.

There is also a possibility that Linda could appeal to the court on the grounds that she and Richard had an implied universal partnership and that she was therefore entitled to half the assets of the partnership when it broke up (see Chapter 8). But again, her application would have to satisfy a number of formal criteria, and her lawyer evidently decided that her case stood little chance of succeeding.

In the end, however, the main argument against using the courts to settle disputes between you and your former partner is that legal disputes are invariably drawn-out and costly affairs. You could easily end up paying more in legal fees than the assets you are fighting over are worth ... and with no guarantee that you will win.

... NOW THE GOOD NEWS

The good news is that the bad news needn't concern you at all if you and your partner work out a fair financial arrangement from the beginning. There are many different ways to do this, and no hard and fast rules: each couple's situation is unique, and a financial arrangement that works well for one couple won't necessarily suit another. Whatever your particular circumstances, you are far more likely to make sound financial decisions and choices if you have realistic expectations about your relationship, know the possible legal implications of your decisions, and talk to each other frankly about money matters.

REALISTIC EXPECTATIONS VS THE 'NEVER-NEVER' SYNDROME

There is nothing more wonderful than being in love. And for many, especially women, there is almost nothing more difficult than facing up to the possibility that their love affair may not last forever. It seems to say, 'I don't trust you, I have no faith in our relationship,' or, even worse, 'I am a shallow, fickle person incapable of lasting love.' The only acceptable attitude is one that says, 'We will never stop loving each other,' 'We will never part.'

Unfortunately, this 'never-never' attitude is seldom based on reality. People do fall out of love. You and your partner may discover after living together for a year that you are totally incompatible. Or one of you may fall in love with someone else. Most live-in relationships don't last – that is a fact, and as Linda's story shows, there is a real risk that you will make bad financial choices if you don't take it into account. Linda's romantic belief that Richard would always be there to take care of her is typical of the 'never-never' syndrome. If instead she had seriously considered what would happen if one day he *wasn't* there, she would have taken steps to ensure that she could cope financially if that day ever came.

By contrast, Olivia and Hans, who lived together for five years before marrying in 1990, 'always operated on the basis that one day we might not be together – we've always been very practical about it.' The way in which she and Hans handle their finances is covered in 'Independence and interdependence' at the end of this chapter. Olivia emphasises that their practical attitude has not in any way lessened their commitment to one another; if anything, it has strengthened it. 'I think the fact that your eyes are wide open makes you try that much harder,' she says.

Admitting there is a chance that you will break up is not the same as desiring it. It is simply an example of rational planning, which we all do as a matter of course in other areas of our lives. When you insure your car against theft, for example, you are not expressing a wish for your car to be stolen. In fact, that is probably the worst-case scenario in your eyes. You are just facing up to a very real possibility and providing yourself with a cushion against the financial blow it would cause.

Unlike car insurance, a sound financial arrangement with your partner needn't cost anything. If your relationship endures – well, that's wonderful. If it doesn't, you will at least have something more than a handful of grocery store till slips with which to begin your life anew.

THE IMPORTANCE OF KNOWING THE LAW

You may think that the way in which you and your partner organise your finances is no one's business but your own. Up to a point you're right: you are perfectly entitled to come to any arrangement that suits you both.

However, there are certain circumstances in which your private affairs, whether you like it or not, may become a matter of concern to others. When this happens, unless you have done some careful and well-informed planning, the decisions you have made together can have legal and financial consequences which you never intended or wanted, and over which you have no control.

Say, for example, that your partner is declared insolvent. If the two of you have always bought furniture and appliances jointly, paying for them by cheque on an account registered in your partner's name, all of these assets will vest in the trustee and may be sold to pay your partner's creditors. If, on the other hand, you have always bought assets separately and have documentary evidence to prove it, only your partner's assets will vest in the trustee. Clearly it is valuable to know this, especially if one of you runs a business; it could have a significant influence on the choices you make regarding your personal finances.

A well-informed decision is better than an uninformed or misinformed decision. Most couples who have a sound financial arrangement have taken the time and effort to acquaint themselves with the law and to think through the possible implications of their choices. This may sound tedious but it can save you a lot of heartache in the long run.

TALKING ABOUT MONEY

It is a common complaint among women that their men don't communicate. 'He bottles everything up', 'he refuses to talk about it when we have a fight', 'he never tells me how he feels' – you've probably heard those or similar moans on countless occasions ... or voiced a few of them yourself. When a number of women get together and the conversation turns to relationships, you can guarantee there will be unanimous agreement that men's reluctance to communicate is a problem, and that communication is absolutely essential to a good relationship.

But ask that same group of women if they communicate frankly with their partners about money and it is just as certain that you will see a large percentage of them starting to backpedal furiously. 'When you love each other, money is irrelevant,' one will say loftily. 'It's so tacky to argue about money,' several others are sure to protest. 'I don't want him to think I'm grasping/mercenary/only in it for the money' and

'I'm terrified of scaring him off' are other likely replies.

Women today can discuss sex with a candour that would make their grandmothers blush, but when it comes to money many of them still show an almost Victorian prudery. The feeling is still widespread, thirty years into the feminist movement, that it is somehow not 'nice' for women to talk about finances, and to many the prospect of a frank discussion with their men about money matters ranks about on a par with having root canal treatment.

This attitude makes no sense, whichever way you look at it. For one thing, resentment over money, if allowed to build up over time, can seriously undermine other areas of your relationship. It is far better for both of you if you discuss financial grievances as they arise and look for a mutually satisfactory solution. The principle here is the same as for any other problem you might have: allowing resentment to simmer is a bad option.

Moreover, an unfair financial arrangement can, as it did in Linda's case, leave one of you with nothing if the relationship ends. Suddenly, money will seem not so irrelevant after all ... but then it is too late to do anything about it.

It is not grasping to take responsibility for yourself and your financial well-being; it is simply mature, sensible behaviour, and there is no reason to feel either guilty or apologetic about doing so. 'Fair', after all, means fair to *both* of you. And the only way you can determine what you both think is fair is to sit down and talk about it. (If your partner is unwilling to discuss a fair financial arrangement with you, you have good reason to ask yourself if your relationship has any future.)

AN ARRANGEMENT TO AVOID

If there is one thing that all live-in partners should avoid, it is a financial arrangement whereby one partner pays the day-to-day living expenses while the other buys the furniture. Such an arrangement may seem simple and convenient but it can have very unfair consequences, as Linda's story shows.

Clearly, if you split up, the one who owns the stove and

microwave oven is in a far better position than the one who bought the food that was cooked in them. Possession is at least nine-tenths of the law, and while your (former) partner may well do the honourable thing and share the assets that were acquired during your relationship, there is no guarantee that this will happen. Furthermore, your ex-partner will be under no legal obligation to reimburse you for all the money you spent on his or her upkeep.

The best arrangement – assuming, of course, that you are both working – is one in which you share day-to-day living expenses and each buy assets separately.

WHAT EXPENSES SHOULD YOU SHARE?

The easiest way to determine what expenses to share is to ask yourselves in each case who benefits. If you both benefit from a particular item, then it is fair to share the cost of it; if only one of you benefits, then it makes sense for only that person to pay.

For example, you obviously both benefit from having water and electricity, whereas only you benefit from your clothes and cosmetics. Similarly, if you don't share your partner's passionate attachment to his three large rottweilers, you have every right to refuse to contribute towards their upkeep. (Of course, they may make you feel more secure, in which case you do benefit.)

Typically, a list of shared expenses might include rent or bond payments; municipal rates; groceries; water, telephone and electricity accounts; salaries for domestic servants; and insurance policies on the house and contents.

However, when you and your partner sit down to draw up your own list, you may find that you want to exclude some of the above items or add others.

Mary runs a catering business from home and the maid spends most of the day helping her in the kitchen, so Mary believes it would be unfair to ask her partner to contribute to the maid's salary. Sandra, who runs a design studio from home, pays the telephone account every month because most of the calls are for her business.

If you both belong to a health club, you may decide to include the membership fees on your list. Liquor bills may become a shared expense if you both enjoy a sundowner, or paid by your partner if he likes expensive scotch and you only drink coke. If your eating habits are the same, it makes sense to share grocery bills; on the other hand, if your own tastes run to *Terrine de poisson au caviar* and your beloved's favourite meal is *slap* chips and a burger, it is probably better if you each pay for your own food!

The possible variations are endless and anything goes, as long as you both agree that it is fair. From a legal point of view, though, it is better if you keep your shared expenses to a minimum and both retain a fair measure of financial independence. This is especially important in the early stages of your relationship, and at any stage if your partner is irresponsible with money.

EQUAL SHARES OR A PRO RATA SPLIT?

Once you have decided what expenses to share, the next thing to consider is: in what proportion will you share them? A 50/50 split is reasonable if your salaries are roughly the same. However, if, as often happens, one of you earns much more than the other, you may agree that this would place too great a financial burden on the lower-paid partner. In your case, sharing expenses pro rata – in other words, in proportion to your respective incomes – may be the fairest solution.

> *Lennie is an attorney with a yearly income of about R75 000. His partner, Nikki, teaches at a government school and earns R25 000 a year. When they decided that Nikki should move in with Lennie, Nikki was determined to pay her 'fair share' – i.e. 50% – of their joint expenses. But Lennie persuaded her that this was completely impractical and, in their case, not fair at all.*
>
> *'She was sharing a flat with two friends when I met her,' he says, 'and paying a few hundred rands rent a month. The rent on my townhouse is over R2 000 a month. Half the rent alone would have taken most of her after-tax salary. I didn't see why she should*

have to pay a financial penalty to live with me; at the same time, I didn't want to move into cheaper accommodation so that she could make the same contribution as me.' They agreed to divide their joint expenses pro rata – Lennie pays 75% of the bills, Nikki 25%.

If your circumstances change significantly – if, for example, you get a promotion with a big salary increase – your pro rata contribution can be adjusted accordingly.

HOW TO PAY

You can, of course, take each bill as it arrives, divide it into two pro rata shares and each write a cheque for your portion. But this is going to involve a lot of cheque-writing and it is very inconvenient for your creditors.

Alternatively, you can each assume responsibility for paying certain accounts if you can divide them into two piles which more or less reflect your respective pro rata share of expenses. The disadvantage of this system is that while some of your expenses are fixed (such as rent and insurance payments), most vary from month to month, and these variable amounts can create inequities. For example, if you divide the accounts into two pro rata shares in the middle of summer, the one who is responsible for the electricity account will end up paying a disproportionate share in winter unless you make a seasonal adjustment.

As a third option, you might consider establishing a joint kitty. South African banks, unlike British banks, do not allow joint accounts, but one of you can open an account and give the other signing powers on it. If you do this, it is always best to retain your own separate accounts and establish a joint kitty by opening a third account.

A joint kitty can simplify your finances considerably and help you to keep track of where your money is going, though it may take you a few months to get it working smoothly. It is also a good way to handle flexible expenses, especially grocery bills, which can add up to a major portion of your living costs.

45

What often happens, if you don't pay for groceries from a joint kitty, is that you and your partner lose track of the R30 here and R70 there that you have each spent on food, and you can both end the month with a vaguely resentful feeling that you have paid more than your share.

The first step is to estimate the total of your shared expenses for the month. This will obviously be a very rough estimate in the beginning, but you can adjust the amount up or down (usually up!) after a few months when you have a clearer idea of your expenses.

Next, calculate how much of that total each of you must contribute, based on whatever pro rata split you have decided is fair. At the end of every month you simply deposit the amount you owe into the account and your partner does the same. Then, because you both have signing powers, either of you can pay the accounts. You may find, however, that you prefer to set aside an evening a month for paying them together. Bill-paying is always a dreary business, but you can reduce the agony if you go out for a leisurely meal first. Signing your money away is less painful on a full stomach and after a bottle of good wine!

Operating a joint kitty does require a certain amount of trust and good faith on both your parts. Because you both have signing powers, either of you can misspend the other's money. Moreover, if the account is registered in your name and you have negotiated an overdraft facility to cover contingencies, you are legally responsible for repaying the bank. So if your partner has a fatal attraction to get-rich-quick schemes or habitually lives beyond his or her means, a joint kitty is not a good idea.

Banks do allow business partners to operate a joint account. According to one bank manager, the bank is not interested in the terms of the partnership and would be happy to open a Smith-Jones Enterprises account for Jane Smith and Bill Jones (provided they both have good financial track records) if that is how they want to handle their shared expenses. One feature of such accounts is that you can require both signatures on cheques if you choose; moreover, both partners are responsible for any overdraft that is incurred – though that is significant only if both partners can be located. It is advisable, if you think this might suit you, to have a frank talk to your bank manager about it.

However you and your partner decide to handle bill-paying, the important thing to remember is that you may need to supply proof of your financial contribution to the household if your relationship should ever end in a legal battle. Say, for example, that you and your partner don't like any of the above options and prefer an arrangement whereby your partner pays all the bills and you reimburse him or her for your share. That's fine, as long as you reimburse your partner by cheque, not in cash, and keep the cancelled cheques.

SAVINGS

From a legal point of view it is wise to have separate savings accounts, even if you are saving for a joint project such as an overseas holiday. If you have one savings account which is registered in your partner's name and he or she is killed in a motorcar accident, that account will become part of the deceased estate; unless your partner has left a will naming you as beneficiary or the two of you have a legal cohabitation contract, you will lose your money.

MAJOR PURCHASES

As stated above, an arrangement whereby one of you pays running costs while the other buys the furniture can have very unfair consequences. If you are sharing running costs, does it also make sense to share the cost of each major purchase? It certainly has practical advantages. Say, for example, that your old fridge is past repair and you need a new one immediately. You want to avoid hire-purchase; neither of you has enough money saved to pay for a new fridge outright, but if you pool your savings you can just manage it.

The trouble is, no matter how fair and convenient it may seem, buying assets jointly is a great way to store up problems for the future. If a year later you decide to end your relationship, who should get the jointly-owned fridge, stereo system or lounge suite? You are both reasonable people, you argue – you would be able to sit down and settle the matter calmly and rationally. Well ... maybe.

But it is far more likely that you won't be feeling either calm or rational when the day comes, and the amicable division of assets that you envisage now could in reality be a bitter, protracted and emotionally draining dispute (and possibly an expensive legal battle). Breaking up is stressful enough without this additional and unnecessary conflict.

Furthermore, jointly-owned assets can pose enormous problems if one of you dies without leaving a will (see Chapter 8).

Altogether, you will make it easier for yourselves in the event that you separate, and easier for your heirs and executors should one of you die intestate, if you purchase assets separately. That way, you leave no room for doubt about which of you owns what. (Buying a house is a special case, as are home improvements. These are dealt with in the following chapter.)

Buying separately can also eliminate a source of conflict within your relationship if – as is often the case – you have different priorities. If you decide, for example, that you need a coffee table and you can afford it, you can simply go and buy one. If you are buying jointly, you could end up arguing with your partner about what is more important – the coffee table, or the new speakers that he or she wants.

Of course, that still doesn't solve the problem of paying for things that you need straight away but don't have the money for. One way to handle this is to make loans to each other as Olivia and Hans do (see below, 'Independence and interdependence').

To establish ownership beyond doubt, it is a good idea to pay for any major items by cheque or credit card and to keep cancelled cheques, credit card slips and receipts in a safe place. This is sound practice in any case as you may need them for insurance purposes or warranty claims. You will also be very glad to have them if your partner is sequestrated.

However practical it may be to buy assets separately, some people just don't feel comfortable about affixing 'his' and 'hers' labels to everything in their home. If you and your partner weigh up the advantages and disadvantages and still decide that you prefer to buy things jointly, it is advisable to draw up a partnership agreement in which you specify how your assets will be divided if you separate (see Chapter 9). In your agreement you could also nominate a person to act as arbitrator – but do clear it with that person first, as it could be a thankless task!

IF YOUR PARTNER IS DECLARED INSOLVENT

The Insolvency Act of 1936 states that if one spouse is sequestrated, the estates of both spouses vest in the trustee. The assets of the solvent spouse must be returned if he or she can prove that they were purchased by his or her own means. But if this cannot be proved, the assets will be sold to pay off creditors.

What does this have to do with you? A lot: the Act defines 'spouse' in such a way that it includes unmarried partners living together as man and wife, unless there is a legal husband or wife. Clearly, then, this is another good reason to keep your assets separate.

TAXATION

Until recently, married couples were subject to joint taxation. This meant that some people – especially high income-earners – had to pay more tax when they married because the wife's income was added to the husband's and taxed at a much higher marginal rate. Many couples were reluctant to pay this financial penalty and chose to live together instead.

However, the Budget of March 1991 finally put an end to joint taxation. The income of a wife (including investment income) will now be taxed completely separately from that of her husband and there should no longer be any significant difference in the total income tax paid by a married as opposed to an unmarried couple. In other words, if avoidance of higher tax was your reason for living together rather than marrying, you can start planning the wedding!

MEDICAL AID SCHEMES

Spouses may be claimed as dependants but live-in partners may not. A marriage certificate is generally required as proof that the member and the dependant are married. If you and your partner have children, either of you may claim the children as dependants for the purpose of medical aid.

IF YOU RUN A BUSINESS TOGETHER

If you and your partner have a joint business venture, it is best to get a lawyer to draw up a partnership agreement in which your respective rights and responsibilities are clearly spelled out. The agreement should also contain a provision to the effect that neither of you can enter into certain transactions without the consent of the other.

The reason such a clause is important is that, by law, if a partnership is dissolved, each partner is liable for all the debts of the partnership. Creditors are under no obligation to sue each of you equally: if your partner disappears, for example, they are entitled to sue you for the entire amount that is owing to them. Of course, once you have repaid all the debts, you have a claim against your former partner – but that is small consolation if he or she cannot be found! A partnership agreement cannot limit your legal responsibility for debts, but it can at least prevent your partner from running up debts without your knowledge and consent.

IF ONLY ONE OF YOU WORKS

Everything that has been said so far applies to couples who both work. This is usually the case, but not always. Some couples have a relationship that resembles a traditional marriage, in which she stays at home while he works. This may be because they have small children or simply because they prefer it that way. Clearly, in such cases, the man pays all the expenses and buys all the assets, unless the woman has some other source of income (e.g. dividends or an inheritance).

What, then, are her rights if their relationship ends? Unfortunately she has virtually none. While spouses are legally obliged to maintain each other, live-in partners are not, and, as mentioned above, the laws that regulate the division of assets upon divorce do not apply to unmarried relationships.

In other words, she is not entitled to any share in the house (unless he has registered it in her name or in both their names) or to any other assets unless she can prove in court that there was an implied universal partnership. Nor is she entitled to maintenance – though he is legally obliged to pay maintenance for any children they might have. Obviously, this can impose severe hardship on some women, especially those who are older, who have been out of the job market for some time, or who have small children.

If you are in this situation, it is a good idea to talk to your partner about getting an attorney to draw up an agreement, or cohabitation contract, between the two of you (see Chapter 9). If he is willing to do so, you will have some measure of protection in the event that your relationship fails – provided, of course, that the courts uphold such a contract. If he *isn't* willing, there is no getting round the fact that your situation is very precarious. It might be wise in that case to take a long hard look at your relationship. At the very least you should consider finding part-time work or taking courses to improve your skills so that you have a better chance of supporting yourself, should the need arise.

If you should become disabled

Married people are legally obliged to maintain their disabled spouses; live-in partners are not. If you become disabled and can no longer support yourself, or face astronomical medical bills, your partner has the legal – if not a moral – right to walk away. For that reason, you might consider taking out a permanent sickness and accident insurance policy. The terms of such policies vary from one insurance company to another, so it is worth checking several of them before you make a decision.

Independence and interdependence

This chapter opened with a tale of woe which is unfortunately very common these days. However, there are many live-in relationships that tell a happier story. Here is one of them.

'If you've been living on your own and financially independent, why should that change just because you're now living with someone?' The question is posed by Olivia, a capable, intelligent young woman of 29 who runs a thriving catering business. She recently married Hans, her live-in partner of five years. Their relationship is a happy combination of independence and interdependence, characterised on the one hand by love, sharing and communication and, on the other, by a fairly businesslike financial arrangement and a high degree of personal financial autonomy.

Looking round their small but beautifully furnished home in Johannesburg's northern suburbs, Olivia remarks that the house belongs to Hans, almost everything in it to her. She explains: 'Hans is European and he believes very strongly that the roof is the man's responsibility. So the house is registered in his name, and everything to do with the house – renovations, the bond, rates, electricity, water and the gardener's salary – are for his account.' She pays for the groceries, pays the maid's salary and the telephone bill, and buys all the furniture, appliances, linen, crockery and kitchen utensils. They share entertainment expenses. They have separate bank accounts and have never had a joint kitty.

This is the system they have had since the day they moved in together; they find it works well and they have seen no reason to change it since they got married. 'Whether you're live-in or married, I think it's absolutely imperative that you retain your financial independence,' says Olivia. For that reason, and also because she is 'terrified of being old and poor', Olivia contributes to a pension plan. 'If Hans and I grow old together – and I hope we will – then we'll both benefit from my pension ... but if for some reason we don't, I know that I'll have enough to live on.'

Olivia stresses the importance of communication. 'Many of my friends believe that Hans and I have the perfect relationship,' she says. 'I tell them that it's not perfect but it's good — and it's good because we work at it and we talk to each other. If we have a problem we discuss it until we've resolved it.' For example, Olivia felt insecure when Hans bought the house before they were married because she knew that if he died intestate, she could suddenly find herself without a roof over her head. She expressed her concern to Hans and 'he was very sympathetic. It was obviously something he'd never considered.' Hans acknowledged her need for security and made a will leaving a half share in the house to her and the other half to relations. (After their marriage he changed his will to make Olivia sole beneficiary. Olivia has also made him sole beneficiary of her will.)

'It's the way you approach a problem that's important,' says Olivia. 'You don't go up to the guy and say, "Listen, if you walk out on me I want the house." If you say to him, "Darling, this makes me feel insecure," he's likely to feel sympathetic and receptive.'

From time to time, because Hans works on commission and Olivia's clients are sometimes late with payments, one of them runs short of money. When that happens they make loans to each other. 'We're very businesslike about it,' says Olivia, 'and we're great believers in writing things down. So we enter the amount in our housekeeping book — we keep track of all our household expenses in it, right down to the R30 spent at the bottle store.' She adds that while they've had their share of arguments, they have 'never, ever fought about money.'

Even though Olivia pays for all the home furnishings, she and Hans always make decisions about purchases jointly — 'including even little things like coffee mugs,' she says. 'We need new mugs now, and if I choose some that he doesn't like, I'll go back and look for others that we're both happy with.'

6

Your home

Whether you and your partner live in a rented flat or buy a house, the home that you share is a major commitment. For one thing, it always involves legal obligations to third parties (landlords, municipalities, banks or building societies), and for that reason alone you cannot afford to be starry-eyed and impractical about it. The other thing is that your mutual home cannot be divided down the middle and shared out if your relationship ends: someone will have to move. So for one of you that very basic necessity – the roof over your head – is now dependent on the success or failure of your emotional relationship.

Clearly, then, your home presents a special set of problems that you need to discuss with each other before you sign a lease or deed of sale. The issues are roughly the same whether you are renting or buying, though they become much more important if you buy property together. They are:

○ What rights (of occupation and ownership) and what responsibilities will each of you have in the home?

○ What will happen if one of you dies, or if one of you wants to end the relationship?

The law has a lot to say about property, and your rights and responsibilities in respect of your home are largely determined as soon as the lease or deed of sale is signed. The first question

that you and your partner have to answer, then, is: who signs
– just one of you, or both?

IF YOU AND YOUR PARTNER ARE RENTING

Most lease agreements today are in the form of a written contract. However, a lease doesn't have to be in writing. In law, a
lease is considered to exist once a landlord and a tenant have
agreed that the tenant will have the use and enjoyment of a
specific property in return for payment of an agreed rent.

The rights and duties of a tenant and his or her landlord are
governed, first of all by the lease agreement between them,
and secondly by the common law. The lease agreement takes
precedence and the common law operates by default. In other
words, you and your landlord are bound by the terms of your
contract of lease, but any matters not covered by the lease are
regulated by the common law.

The terms of a lease agreement are often different from the
common law. For example, the common law states that if
there is more than one lessee, in the absence of agreement to
the contrary, joint liability applies: in other words, each tenant
is liable only for his or her share of the rent. However, many
lease agreements today state that joint tenants are jointly and
severally liable: that is, each may be held liable for the whole
amount of the rent.

A lease may stipulate that it will terminate on the death of
the tenant, whereas the common law rule, if the lease is silent
on this subject, is that the rights and obligations arising from
the lease pass to the deceased tenant's heirs.

Clearly, it is important to read the terms of your lease agreement carefully and to take note of what isn't covered as well as
what is. If you want to know more about the common law
rights and duties of landlords and tenants, check the reference
section of your local library. One of the best books on the
subject is *The South African Law of Landlord and Tenant* by
W.E. Cooper (Juta, 1973).

Both a joint tenancy lease and a sole tenancy lease have advantages and disadvantages for a live-in couple. However,

you can minimise the disadvantages in either case with a private agreement between the two of you.

Joint tenancy

If you both sign the lease, you are joint tenants. This means that you both have security of tenure – that is, the right to live in the flat – and you are both legally responsible for paying the rent for the duration of the lease.

This is fine as long as you remain together – but what happens if your relationship ends before the lease does? You are both entitled to remain in the flat, but one of you will have to move out. Which one will it be? Furthermore, the partner who moves out is still legally liable for his or her share of the rent until the lease expires. If the lease stipulates joint and several liability and the partner who remains in the flat defaults for any reason, the landlord has the right to demand payment of all the rent money owed from the one who left.

That is why a private agreement is important. In it, you and your partner can state which of you will move in the event that you break up. Let's say that you will leave and your partner will remain. To protect you, the agreement should also contain a clause in which your partner indemnifies you against any further liability for rent after you have left. This agreement should be in writing and signed by both of you. It does not give you ironclad protection, because the landlord isn't bound by it. He can still claim the rent (or your portion of the rent) from you if your partner defaults. But if you do have to pay the landlord, you then have a legal claim against your former partner.

If your partner dies, you have the right to remain in the flat until the lease expires. Depending on the terms of the lease, you may become liable for the entire rent or, if your partner's obligations have passed to his or her estate, you will be obliged to pay a half share as before.

If, as often happens, one of you is already living in a rented flat which you both like when you decide to live together, you can ask the landlord to draw up a new joint tenancy lease to replace the existing sole tenancy agreement. Landlords are usually happy to oblige, especially if the joint tenancy lease stipulates joint and several liability – they then have two people to chase after for the rent instead of just one. You will have to pay stamp duty on the new lease, but unless it is a long lease at a high rent, this will not be a significant amount.

Alternatively, you may decide to keep the existing sole tenancy lease.

Sole tenancy

If you want to keep the existing sole tenancy lease, check its terms carefully first. It may contain a clause prohibiting occupation of the rented premises by any person other than the sole tenant. It is not a good idea to ignore this: if the landlord discovers that you are both living in the flat, he has the right to terminate the lease. If your lease does include such a clause, you can ask the landlord either to draw up a new joint tenancy lease or waive the restriction.

If he agrees orally to waive the restriction, check your lease again! If it contains a non-variation clause, an oral waiver is not sufficient. A non-variation clause, which is common in leases, generally goes something like this: 'No variation of the terms and conditions of this contract shall be of any force and effect unless reduced to writing and signed by both lessor and lessee.'

But this is not the only problem with a sole tenancy lease. Let's assume that the lease is in your partner's name. This means that you have neither legal responsibilities nor rights with regard to the flat. The fact that you are not liable for rent is to your advantage: if your relationship is short-lived and you move out, there won't be any of the unpleasant financial repercussions that are possible with a joint tenancy lease. On the other hand, you have no security of tenure and this puts you at an enormous disadvantage. Your partner has the legal right to evict you at any time, and if he or she is unreasonable, that time could be in the middle of the night after a quarrel.

To give you some protection, you and your partner might consider entering into a written agreement in which he or she promises to give you a reasonable length of time – a month, say – to find alternative accommodation if your relationship breaks down. The question is: will this be of any value to you in the middle of the night during a heated row? It is doubtful whether waiving a written agreement at such a time will make your partner calm down and see reason. It is far more likely to enrage him or her even further. If that is the case, you will need a court order to enforce your rights – and unfortunately they just aren't available at a moment's notice.

If your partner dies and his or her sole tenancy agreement states that it will terminate in the event of death, the landlord is entitled to insist that you vacate the flat. In practice, however, this doesn't usually happen. Unless the landlord wants to sell the flat or has some other reason for wanting to repossess it, he will probably give you the opportunity to rent the flat in your name.

Subletting your own flat

If you are moving into your partner's home but have doubts about your relationship, it might be a good idea to hang on to your own flat just in case. Check the terms of your lease to see if it prohibits subletting. If it doesn't, you are entitled to find a subtenant. Almost all leases today require the written consent of the landlord for subletting, but they often state that 'such consent shall not be unreasonably withheld'. Remember, though, that you are still legally responsible for paying the rent to your landlord if your subtenant defaults.

IF YOU BUY A HOUSE

In the long run it usually makes good sense financially to own the house you live in. It is also very satisfying emotionally. However, a house is the single most expensive purchase most of us ever make, and it is extremely important to consider the questions at the beginning of this chapter – what rights and responsibilities will each of you have in the property, and what will happen if your relationship ends or one of you dies – very carefully before signing a deed of sale.

These questions seem fairly straightforward and uncomplicated, but they represent what a Johannesburg conveyancer
calls a 'minefield of potential problems'. With careful planning
and legal advice you can reduce the risks involved. Unfortunately, you can't eliminate them.

The significance of registration

The most important thing to know about buying immovable
property is that according to the law, the *prima facie* (i.e. on
first impression) *owner of a property is the person who is named in
the registered title deed as the owner*. If both your names are entered in the deed of transfer registered in the deeds registry,
you are joint legal owners of the property. If only one person's
name is entered in the title deed – let's say it is your partner's
name – then your partner is *prima facie* the sole legal owner of
the property even if he or she has signed a separate private contract with you stating that you own the property jointly (see
'Private contracts to own property jointly' below).

When you buy a house, therefore, the first thing you and
your partner have to decide is whether you want the house to
be registered in both your names or in one name only. This
decision must be made before signing the deed of sale, because
the seller's conveyancer will prepare and execute the deed of
transfer to convey the property to the buyer or buyers named
in the deed of sale. If only one of you signs the deed of sale and
you decide the following day that you want the property to be
transferred to both of you, the deed of sale will have to be
amended to reflect that you are purchasing the property
jointly.

However, an amendment to a deed of sale requires the seller's permission; if the seller refuses to allow the change, you
are unfortunately stuck with the original terms of the sale. If
he does agree to the amendment, you can either have the entire
deed of sale re-written, which will be expensive, or enter into
an addendum agreement, which is cheaper and serves the same
purpose.

Joint ownership

The advantage of pooling your resources to buy a house is that you will be able to buy a better house than either of you could afford on your own. Very often, in fact, it means the difference between buying and not buying at all. House prices and bond rates are so high that few individuals can afford to carry all the costs alone.

In recent years there has been a marked increase in the number of house sales to live-in couples. A conveyancer in Johannesburg's northern suburbs estimates that 25% of his clients in 1990 were unmarried couples, and he adds that most of them chose to be registered as joint owners.

The disadvantages of joint ownership are discussed below.

Joint ownership needn't be in equal shares

Joint ownership doesn't necessarily mean equal shares. Property (except agricultural land, which may not be registered in more than one name) can be owned by two or more people in any ratio. For example, if Jane Smith has R30 000 to put down as a deposit and her partner Bill Jones has R70 000, they can become owners of 30% and 70% of the property respectively. This information must also be written in the deed of sale. The title deed registered in the deeds registry will then state that the owners are 'Jane Smith as to three-tenths and Bill Jones as to seven-tenths'. When Jane and Bill sell the house, Jane will receive 30% of the net proceeds and Bill 70%.

In most cases your share, as in the example above, will be based on the amount of money you have to put into the property. But it doesn't have to be. Perhaps you have R30 000 to invest and your partner has R70 000, but your partner decides you should each have a half share in the house. Or perhaps you have no capital at all to invest, but again your partner generously decides to make you a joint owner in some ratio. (Obviously your partner will consider doing this only if your relationship is stable and happy and likely to last.)

By law, a person may make donations of up to R20 000 in a

year without paying donations tax. If the donation exceeds R20 000, donations tax of 15% is payable on the excess. In other words, R4 500 tax will be payable on a donation of R50 000. This is a lot of money and no doubt you would far rather use it to furnish or improve your new home than pay it to the Receiver of Revenue. A better arrangement, if an amount greater than R20 000 is involved, is for your partner to donate the first R20 000 to you and lend you the balance. In each year that follows, your partner can donate to you R20 000 of the amount outstanding on the loan until the loan is discharged.

Obtaining a bond

Banks and building societies today tend to treat a bond application by an unmarried couple in the same way as an application by a husband and wife married with an antenuptial contract. If you both have a steady source of income and a good credit record, they will generally take both your incomes into consideration in calculating the amount they are willing to lend. Most use the rule that monthly bond repayments should not exceed 30% of monthly income. For example, if you and your partner have a combined monthly income of R4 500, your monthly bond repayment should not be higher than R1 350. With the bond rate currently hovering around 20%, this means that the maximum you may borrow is about R81 000.

It is important to note that most institutions will take both your incomes into consideration only if the house is registered in both your names. In this respect you are treated differently from married couples: normally both their incomes will be taken into account even if the house is registered in only one name.

Sharing costs

The fairest arrangement, if you are joint owners, is to share all costs related to the property in the same ratio in which you own it. In other words, if you each own a half share, then it is reasonable for each of you to pay half the expenses. If you own 30% of the property and your partner owns 70%, a corresponding 30%/70% division of expenses is fair. (Of course, this is possible only if you both have an income. If for any reason one of you has no income, all the costs will have to be paid by the other.)

These costs include anything that is directly relevant to your investment: bond repayments, comprehensive house-owner's insurance, renovations, additions, repairs, pool maintenance, security, paving and landscaping.

Problems of joint ownership

Serious problems can arise if your relationship ends, or if one of you defaults on payments, is declared insolvent, or dies.

If your relationship ends

Suppose you decide after a year or two that you no longer love your partner and want to end the relationship. You haven't entered into an agreement about what will happen if you break up, but you're both reasonable people and you don't anticipate a problem. So you suggest to your partner that the house be sold and that you both go your separate ways. Your partner refuses to consider putting the house on the market. You then offer to sell your share in the house to your partner. Again your partner refuses. Feeling desperate now, you offer to buy his or her share, even though you don't know how you would manage to pay for it. Another refusal.

Without a prior legally enforceable agreement you cannot force your partner to accept any one of these options. As joint owners, you both have the right to occupy the home. Neither of you can evict the other or compel the other to agree to sell the property. This is true even if you own the property in a 10%: 90% ratio – the principle of majority rule doesn't apply. The only course of action left to you then is to ask the court to settle the matter.

The most recent reported case involving joint owners who were unable to agree on the disposition of their jointly owned

62

property was heard in 1984. The case involved seven co-owners, six of whom were in agreement that the property should be sold to a certain buyer. The seventh co-owner refused to grant his permission to the sale because he wanted to buy the property himself. In ruling that the seventh co-owner should be allowed to buy the property, the judge quoted from AJ Oosthuizen's *The Law of Property* (Juta, Cape Town, 1981, p 63), which states:

> The Court has a wide discretion ... and may make such order as appears to be fair and equitable in the circumstances ... if the property is indivisible, the Court may award it to one of the joint owners subject to the payment of compensation to the others; or it may order the property to be sold by public auction and the proceeds to be divided among the joint owners in accordance with their shares.

Of course, getting a court ruling is neither quick nor cheap. It could be two years or more before your case is heard, and because it must be heard by the Supreme Court it could end up costing in the region of R50 000 to R60 000. However, if the judge believes your partner has necessitated the court case by acting unreasonably, he may order your partner to pay the costs.

This happened in a case in 1943 involving three properties in Benoni. The properties had been owned jointly by two men, Carl Rother and Samuel Sandig. Both men died, and the executors of Sandig's deceased estate found it impossible to deal with Mrs Rother, who was administrator of her deceased husband's estate. She obstructed all their attempts to end the co-ownership of the properties and they finally asked the court for a ruling. The judge ordered the sale of the properties by public auction and ordered Rother's estate to pay the costs.

(Arguably you have an alternative to petitioning the court, and that is to sell your share in the undivided property to someone else. But how are you going to market it, and who is going to buy it? Even if you are able to find a buyer, which is extremely unlikely, your half share in the property will sell for substantially less than you would receive for it if the entire property were sold. Moreover, you could still end up in a legal battle with your partner. The reason is that while a co-owner is entitled to sell his share in a jointly owned property without the other co-owner's permission, a party to a partnership cannot. Your live-in partner could argue that the two of you had an unwritten partnership agreement and that therefore his or her permission is required for the sale of your half share.)

Obviously you don't want to find yourself in this situation, and fortunately it can be avoided if you and your partner enter into a separate legal agreement when you buy the house. The agreement should state that, if for any reason either of you should wish to sell your share of the property, the other must buy it, failing which the property as a whole will be sold. This agreement should be in writing and signed by both of you.

If you and your partner have entered into such a contract and then your partner still refuses either to buy your share or to agree to the sale of the house, you can apply to the Supreme Court for an order for specific performance. In other words, you can ask the court to order your partner to comply with the terms of the agreement. This is quicker and much cheaper than the procedure described above; moreover, if you win the case your partner will be directed to pay the costs and you will recover most (about 70%) of your expenses. You can keep costs to a minimum by including in your agreement a clause that in the event of a dispute you agree to submit to the jurisdiction of the magistrate's court (which involves much less expense than the Supreme Court) in the district in which you reside.

If one of you defaults on payments

If you are both registered owners of the property, the bond will also be registered in both your names. It doesn't matter in what ratio you and your partner own the house, or in what ratio you have agreed to be responsible for costs: the bond will state that the bank or building society holds you jointly and severally liable for the whole amount of the bond. If your partner defaults on his or her share of the bond repayments, the bank can sue you both and obtain judgement from the court for payment of the full amount outstanding on the mortgage loan. The bank will usually at the same time obtain a court order authorising the sale of the property to recover the judgement debt. This is the procedure known as foreclosure.

Banks would rather avoid foreclosure if possible, so even after court judgement has been obtained you may be able to stop the sale of your house by paying all the arrears and convincing the bank that you will continue to pay bond instalments fully and promptly in future. The bank may be willing to help you by altering the terms of your bond; for example, it may agree to amortise your loan over a longer period so that your monthly instalments are lower. However, it is obviously not a good idea to wait for the bank to initiate legal proceedings before you take steps to remedy the situation. Your best plan is to make sure that your partner does not default, if necessary by paying his or her share of the bond repayments yourself, and to speak to the bank about the problem as soon as possible.

Here again, a written and signed legal agreement between you and your partner is useful. In it you should state in what ratio you have agreed to share costs associated with the house. This agreement is not binding on the bank or building society. However, if your partner defaults on his or her agreed share of the bond repayments and you end up paying his or her share yourself in order to avoid foreclosure, you have a claim against your partner.

An agreement of this nature is not strictly necessary because you would have a claim in any case. According to the law, 'each co-owner is liable for a share in the expenses and losses which the running and the upkeep of the property involves and if one has paid all expenses he may recover the other's share'. (*The Law of Property*, Silberberg and Schoeman, Butterworth, 1983, p. 334.) However, it serves as proof of your financial arrangement and will strengthen your hand in the event of a dispute. You might also consider including in this agreement a provision that if either partner fails to pay his or her share of the mortgage payments, say, twice in succession, he or she will agree to sell to the other partner his or her share of the property.

If one of you is declared insolvent

Sequestration of your partner's estate invariably leads to extremely messy and unpleasant complications in your life. First of all, the Insolvency Act defines spouse in such a way that it includes a woman who is living with a man as his wife or a man who is living with a woman as her husband. According to the Act, the estates of both spouses, so defined, vest in the trustee of the insolvent estate.

The property of the solvent spouse will be released only if he or she can prove that the property legitimately belongs to him or her. In other words, if you are living together as man and wife you will have to prove that your share in the jointly owned house was acquired by your own means, otherwise it will be sold by the trustee to pay your partner's creditors. This is one reason why it is extremely important to be seen to be paying all costs associated with the property in the same ratio in which you own it.

Let's assume that you can prove your share in the house is legitimately yours. Let's also assume that you have somehow managed to avoid defaulting on the bond repayments, rates, etc. as a result of your partner's ever-worsening financial difficulties prior to sequestration. If you have avoided default by paying all your partner's bills yourself, you are also one of his or her creditors. However, you are ranked as a concurrent creditor and the trustee will consider concurrent claims only after he has paid the costs of sequestration and the claims of all the secured and preferential creditors. By that stage, of course, there may well be nothing left in the estate.

In the meantime, what has happened to your jointly owned house? The trustee has a duty to the creditors to realise as much as he can on your partner's share in the property, so as a first step he will probably ask you if you are willing to buy your partner's share at half the market value of the property as a whole. If you do not want, or cannot afford, to do this, he will probably ask you to agree to the sale of the property. If you aren't willing to do this either, he will have no option but to try to sell your partner's share in the undivided property.

It is extremely unlikely that he will find a buyer – though if the house offers the possibility of a good return you could conceivably find yourself one day co-owning the house with XYZ Property Investments. You might try to find a buyer for your partner's share – your parents or a friend, for example, with whom you wouldn't mind being co-owner. Alternatively, you could sit back and wait for the trustee to come back to you and ask you to make him an offer, in which case you would be able to purchase the other half of your house at a bargain price.

If one of you dies

If your partner dies and leaves his or her share in the property to you in a will, the only problem you might face is that you may not be able to carry all the costs on your own. However, this problem need never arise. As soon as you and your partner obtain a bond on the house, you should each take out a life assurance policy on the other's life for the value of the bond. (The fact that you are co-owners of real property gives you a legitimate insurable interest in each other – see Chapter 8.) It is a good idea to take cover in the policy for permanent disability as well.

In that way, if your partner dies and leaves his or her share in the house to you, you will at the same time receive enough money from the insurance to pay off the bond in its entirety and own the house free and clear. Of course, you will be paid out by the insurance company regardless of the terms of your partner's will. Thus even if your partner leaves his or her share in the house to someone else, you will have enough money either to offer to buy that person out or to purchase another property. If your partner should become permanently disabled, you can pay off the bond with the insurance money and that will make it much easier for the two of you to live on one salary.

Life assurance policies on healthy young people are quite inexpensive. Here, for example, are some rates quoted by a reputable insurance company: To insure the life of a male non-smoker aged 30 for R100 000 will cost approximately R28 a month. Disability cover will cost an additional R8 per month. Premiums for smokers are loaded by 20%, and high blood pressure or other health problems will result in further loading of the premiums. It is cheaper to insure a woman's life: under R22 a month for R100 000 coverage on a 30-year-old non-smoker. Disability cover for women, at just under R10 a month, is slightly higher than for men because of risks associated with pregnancy and childbirth. For double the cover, you will pay double the premiums.

If you and your partner subsequently sell the house and end your relationship, you can still keep up the policy on your partner's life, even though you no longer have an insurable interest in him or her. The only requirement is that an insurable interest must have existed at the time the policy was taken out. However, it probably makes more sense for you and your partner to cede your policies to each other. You can do this by means of a cession, which is a legal document transferring ownership to another. That way, each of you will become the legal owner of a policy on your own life when you part.

As an alternative to insuring each other's lives, you can each insure your own life and cede the policy to your partner. If your relationship ends, you can agree to cancel the cessions. A third option is for each of you to insure your own life and name your partner as beneficiary of the policy. However, this does not offer you the same security as either of the above options. The reason is that either of you can change your beneficiary at any time without the other's knowledge.

What happens if your partner wills his or her share in the house to some other person? This could have very unpleasant consequences for you, especially if that person exercises his or her right, as co-owner, to occupy the house. But it could be worse: it could be half a dozen people. Let's say your partner left his or her share in the house to three cousins and their wives who have recently arrived from Bulgaria, and they all decide to move into the house with their numerous boisterous offspring. This is very unlikely, of course, but stranger things have happened.

Sharing occupation isn't the only problem: now that the three cousins and their wives are all co-owners with you, the consent of all six of them is required for the sale of the house. If you don't want to live with them, they won't sell you their share, they can't afford to buy your share, and they refuse to put the house on the market, you are back to the situation described above (in 'If your relationship ends') of having to ask the court to settle the dispute.

Is it not possible to prevent such a situation by entering into a contract with your partner in which each of you agrees to bequeath your share in the house to the other, or in which you at the very least agree that certain people will not inherit? Unfortunately, the law does not permit limitations on an individual's right to free testation. In other words, such a contract is invalid unless you both retain the right to revoke your promise unilaterally at any time.

If your partner dies without leaving a will, his or her share in the house will be disposed of according to the Intestate Succession Act. You could easily end up co-owning the house with your partner's widowed mother, four brothers and sisters and three step-brothers from his or her deceased father's previous marriage. Of course, people are generally reasonable, and chances are that you will all be able to come to a mutually satisfactory agreement about the property. In all likelihood they will agree to sell their shares in the house to you – particularly if you can offer cash, thanks to the insurance policy you took out on your partner's life. But there is always a possibility that someone will be difficult, and in that case you could – yet again – find yourself back in court.

Private contracts to own property jointly

Sandra and Colin have been living together for about five years. Both earn high incomes, Sandra as a self-employed graphic designer and Colin as a financial adviser. About two years ago they had a house built for them at a cost of R300 000. The bank for which Colin works has a bond subsidy scheme for employees, and Colin qualified for a bond of R200 000 at 10% interest. At half the going rate, this represented a significant saving. However, there was a condition attached to the loan: the house had to be registered in Colin's name.

Understandably, they were both eager to take advantage of the bond subsidy. At the same time, Sandra wanted to be co-owner of the house and to contribute equally to all expenses. So they agreed that the house would be registered in Colin's name, but that they would draw up a private contract stating that the property has been purchased by them jointly and that they are accordingly joint owners.

As stated in their agreement, Sandra pays half of all the expenses relating to the property. She put down half the deposit, pays half the bond, and also pays half the perks tax that Colin pays on the bond subsidy. 'Anything that is relevant to our investment – the outside wall, the instant lawn – we write down and divide the cost by two,' she says.

Colin adds, 'We want a long future together. We wouldn't have gone into all this otherwise. But if we ever did split up, I think we'd be mature enough to settle everything amicably. We have absolute faith in each other.'

Absolute faith is certainly what is needed – not on Colin's part, but on Sandra's. What she is doing is contributing half the money towards the purchase of a house of which Colin is the sole legal owner. No matter what private agreement she and Colin might come to, the law states that *the owner of a property is the person who is registered as the owner.*

The justification for this is that third parties often need to know who owns a particular property. If you offer your house as collateral for a loan, for example, the bank must be able to ascertain that you are in fact the owner of the house. Banks and building societies are involved in thousands of transactions like this every day, and their task would be very difficult if the law allowed private agreements to override the information on property ownership that is recorded in the deeds registry.

As registered owner, Colin has real rights in the property that he can enforce against the whole world – he can occupy it, sell it or bequeath it as he chooses. Sandra, on the other hand, has paid the same amount of money but all she has is a contract which gives her little more than the right to go to court should Colin renege on any of its terms. She cannot enforce the terms of the contract against anyone except Colin.

The implications of such an arrangement can be extremely serious. For example, if Colin becomes insolvent and his estate is sequestrated, the entire property will vest in the trustee and may be sold to pay his creditors. The contract makes Sandra one of his creditors, but her claim will be considered only after secured and preferential claims have been paid. She may well end up receiving nothing.

Furthermore, Colin can sell the property without her consent, and he will receive all the proceeds of the sale because he is sole registered owner. If this happens, Sandra has an action against him for breach of contract – but of course this takes time and money to pursue.

Unfortunately, as long as perks are not fully taxed, many couples are likely to take their chances with this sort of arrangement in order to benefit from a subsidised bond scheme. But in every case, the one whose name does not appear in the title deed to the property is making what could prove to be a very expensive mistake.

Buying a share in your partner's property

It may be that your partner already owns a house when the two of you meet, and that you move into the house. If at some future stage you want to buy a share in the house and your partner is agreeable, this is not difficult to arrange. First of all, your partner must record in writing that he or she is selling

71

you an undivided half (or third, or quarter, or whatever the case may be) share in the property. Let's say the property is worth R200 000 and you are purchasing a half share. You must then pay transfer duty on the value of the half share, i.e. on half of R200 000. This will come to R2 700. You will also have to pay a conveyancing fee.

If there is no bond on the property, that is all that is required. However, if there is a bond the bank must give its written consent to the transfer. This is because as a rule no transfer of a share of mortgaged land is permitted unless the share is released from the operation of the bond. If the bond is very small in relation to the value of the property, the bank will probably grant its consent. However, if the bond is for a large amount the bank will insist that the old bond be cancelled and that a new bond be registered in both names.

If one of you is sole owner

Let's say your partner is sole owner of the house in which you both live. Firstly, if you are working, it is only fair to pay your partner rent. The two of you will have to come to an agreement about what is a reasonable amount. However, it is not a good idea for you to pay for capital improvements to the property. If you want to make a greater contribution to the home than just the rent, you should rather buy furniture or appliances that you need. You can both enjoy the use of these while you are together, but if your relationship ends you can take them with you.

The problem with living in your partner's house is that, for all practical purposes, you have no rights in the property whatsoever. It can be argued that you are your partner's tenant (because you are paying rent) and that you have a periodic monthly lease which gives you the right at common law to a month's notice if your partner wishes to terminate the lease. However, this right is of questionable value to you because it would be costly and time-consuming to enforce. The fact is that if your partner sells the property without your knowledge or decides to evict you, you have little meaningful recourse.

72

For what it's worth, you might ask your partner to agree in writing to give you a reasonable length of time (say one to two months) to find somewhere else to live if your relationship breaks down.

Joint ownership of property via a company or close corporation

Land that is classified as agricultural may not be registered in more than one name. Smallholdings often fall into this category. If you and your partner want to purchase an agricultural property jointly, the only way you can do so is by forming a company or close corporation (CC) and buying the smallholding in the name of this entity. Any property, in fact, can be purchased in this way.

The disadvantage of buying through a corporate entity is that it is expensive. Firstly, it will cost you about six to seven hundred rands to register the CC (unless you do it yourself). It will cost even more to register a company. Secondly, you will have to pay transfer duty of 5% on the full purchase price, as opposed to the normal rate of 1% on the first R30 000 and 3% on the balance. If the selling price of the smallholding or house is R300 000, for example, the transfer duty will be R15 000, compared to R8 400 if one of you had bought the same property as a private individual.

However, ownership via a CC has several advantages that may make this initial cost worthwhile in your case. It is extremely flexible because you can adjust ownership of the property simply by changing the membership of the CC. This can be done quickly, cheaply and easily. Say, for example, that you and your partner decide after a year to part company. Your partner's brother wants to buy your share of the property. All you have to do is sell your share in the CC to the brother. Because ownership of the *property* hasn't been transferred – the property is still registered in the name of the CC – neither transfer duty nor conveyancing fees have to be paid. The only expense involved is a legal fee of about two hundred rands to register an amendment to the CC agreement.

Alternatively, say you and your partner want to start a business together and need capital. You can sell a share in the CC to a third party who will put up the capital. Once again, no transfer duty or conveyancing fees are payable. If you want to sell the entire property, you simply sell the CC. Thus, while the initial costs of a CC are high, subsequent costs can be much lower than with conventional ownership.

7

If you have a child

Paul and Eileen had been living together almost three years when she became pregnant. Their relationship had been stormy for some time and the pregnancy was unintended, but when Eileen gave birth to a son they were both thrilled. Paul proved to be a wonderful father, and after Eileen returned to work three months later, he usually bathed and changed the baby and played with him every evening while she made dinner.

However, Paul and Eileen were arguing more and more, and despite regular sessions with a counsellor they weren't able to resolve their differences. Finally, when James was ten months old, Eileen moved out. A week later Paul phoned her at work to ask if he could pick up James on Sunday morning to take him round to his parents for lunch, as they had done most Sundays in the past. Though his parents had never approved of his live-in relationship, they doted on their grandson – their first – and looked forward to seeing him every weekend. Paul was thunderstruck when Eileen told him she would not allow him to see his baby any more. Furthermore, she informed him, she had instituted proceedings to obtain child maintenance from him.

Paul was angry and upset but he was convinced Eileen had no right to deny him access to James. After all, he had acknowledged paternity to the Registrar of Births, and James had his surname. Anyway, he reasoned, surely if he was required to pay maintenance he must have a right to see his child. So he contacted an attorney – who brusquely set him straight. The father of an il-

legitimate child, he was told, has no paternal authority and consequently no right of access. Eileen was acting entirely within her legal rights. As for Paul – he had no rights.

The price of ignorance of the law in this case was heartbreak, not just for Paul but also for his parents. Though Paul faithfully pays maintenance and he and his parents send birthday and Christmas presents for James, Eileen has denied every request for a visit and they have not seen the little boy in over two years. Paul is extremely bitter, but most of his anger now is directed against himself. His terse advice to other men whose partners become pregnant, or who are contemplating having a child with their partners – get married.

THE MOTHER HAS SOLE CUSTODY AND GUARDIANSHIP…

If any of the facts in the above story were different – if Paul didn't love his son, if Eileen had been more accommodating, if they had parted on good terms – the effect of the law would not have been so harsh. But the fact is, the law was intended to be harsh. The Dutch jurists whose writings form the basis of South Africa's Roman-Dutch law believed that the father who did not wish to make his child legitimate by marrying the mother should be punished. That is why the usual principle that there should be a right corresponding to every duty does not apply in this case: the father has the duty to maintain his illegitimate child, but no corresponding rights.

When a married couple has a child, both the mother and the father have parental power – in other words, they both have rights and obligations towards the child. These are usually referred to as custody and guardianship. Custody, which is shared by married parents, involves the child's day-to-day protection, nourishment, discipline, education and religious instruction. The father of a child born in marriage has guardianship, which means that he manages the child's property and investments and represents the child in any legal proceedings. As the father also has the final say if he and the mother disagree on a matter related to their child's welfare, his rights and duties are somewhat greater than the mother's.

In the case of a child born out of marriage, however, the mother is both custodian and guardian, the only exception being that if she is a minor, her own guardian will normally be the child's guardian until she comes of age. The child takes the mother's nationality and place of domicile, and she alone has the right to choose the child's first name or names.

... EVEN IF THE FATHER ACKNOWLEDGES PATERNITY

Many men assume, as Paul did, that if the natural father acknowledges paternity and registers the infant in his name, he acquires the same rights as a married father. He doesn't. Virtually the only way he can obtain parental power over his child is by marrying the child's mother. However, he will become the child's guardian if the mother dies and names him as guardian in her will (subject to the approval of the Supreme Court, which is the upper guardian of all minors).

If he believes that his former partner is abusing or neglecting their child, he can ask the court to give him custody or to make him the child's legal guardian – but so can any person with an interest in the child. The court will then decide whether it is in the child's best interest to grant his request. However, an experienced social worker at Child Welfare says that to her knowledge, guardianship has never been awarded to the father of an illegitimate child.

WHAT THIS MEANS IN TERMS OF ADOPTION AND ACCESS

The mother of an extramarital child may put the baby up for adoption without the father's consent or even his knowledge. He has no rights in the matter whatsoever. Furthermore, existing law prohibits the father from adopting his own illegitimate child. However, this will probably change soon. An amendment to the Child Care Act which would permit the father of an illegitimate child to adopt his offspring is presently

77

at the bill stage – in other words, it has been formally proposed but not yet passed into legislation.

The law is less clear on the question of the father's right of access. *The Law of Persons and the Family* (P.Q.R. Boberg, Juta & Co Ltd, 1977) states that the father of an extramarital child has a right of 'reasonable access'. Access was considered by the South African Law Commission when it investigated the legal position of illegitimate children in 1985. In its report the Commission said:

> It appears that the direction in which the law is tending is to grant the father access to his illegitimate child, although some would allow this only on an order of court. If the father's sense of responsibility is fostered by access, he could be persuaded to support the child adequately. Furthermore the child might need a father figure ... on the other hand it might be undesirable for the father to exercise his right of access in certain cases. The present question is whether he must be able to exercise it automatically, the court being able to deprive him of it in appropriate cases, or whether he should be able to exercise it only with the Court's approval ... Since legal development is tending in the right direction, it is undesirable for the legislature to interfere at this stage.

Since the report was published, however, the courts seem to have moved in the opposite direction entirely. In 1987 the father of an illegitimate son asked the Zimbabwe High Court to grant him access to his child. The man had admitted paternity and was paying maintenance willingly. In giving his ruling the judge stated: 'My conclusion is that there is no inherent right of access or custody for a father of a minor illegitimate child but the father, in the same way as other third parties, has a right to claim and will be granted these if he can satisfy the Court that it is in the best interests of the child.' The judge refused access on the grounds that the man had not proved it was in the boy's interests.

In another case heard in Natal in 1988 the mother and father of the child had been living together at the time of his birth but had parted when he was about 18 months old. After allowing the father access for several months, the mother had decided to end all contact between them. She had subsequently married.

The judge denied the father's request for access, giving his reasons as follows: The father of a legitimate child 'has a right of access of which he will only be deprived in exceptional cases.' The father of an illegitimate child, by contrast, 'has no right of access and he will not be granted such a right "unless there is some very strong ground compelling [the Court] to do so." ' In other words, the Court 'will only interfere with the *de jure* position in exceptional cases in which considerations relating to the interests of the child compel it to do so.' There were no compelling reasons for granting the father access in this case; on the contrary, the judge believed that if the father were granted access, the child would become the 'victim of acrimony' between his mother and father and 'this will be immeasurably more harmful to him than the permanent severance of the bond between him and applicant [i.e. his father].'

Finally, access was denied in a case heard in the Witwatersrand Local Division in 1990. The judge stated that access is an 'incidence or consequence of parental authority' and that as the father had not acquired parental authority (i.e. by marrying the mother of the child), he had no right of access. He also emphasised that a 'right of access is not a *quid pro quo* for payment of maintenance.'

Our courts have therefore taken a much harder line than English courts, which for some years have leaned toward the view that it is usually in the child's best interests to see both parents. In 1977 the English judge Sir George Baker stated that '... a court should be extremely slow to shut out either parent when the parents and child have lived together under the same roof.'

An organisation called The Unmarried Father's Fight, or TUFF, was formed in Durban in 1990 by a number of unmarried fathers whose former partners have denied them access. They believe that while the law is fair in regard to fathers who evade their maintenance obligations and are not willing to accept parental responsibilities, it unfairly penalises those who care and provide financially for their children.

TUFF is lobbying for changes to the law that would give a 'participating father' of an extramarital child the same rights as a divorced father. This would mean that a participating father's consent would be required before the child could be adopted, he would automatically become the child's guardian if the mother died, and he would have a legal right to reasonable access.

The South African Law Commission announced a new investigation into the question of access at the beginning of 1991. Its report and recommendations should be available before the end of the year.

In the meantime, the mother's rights in relation to adoption and access can lead in extreme cases to ugly emotional blackmail.

Steven and Lisa split up shortly after their daughter was born. At first, Lisa allowed him to see the baby every weekend, but then she started threatening to put the child up for adoption if Steven didn't pay more maintenance. He increased his payments by R100 a month, but a few months later she renewed her threat and asked for a further increase. Steven has agreed to pay the higher amount, but he knows he is in a classic no-win situation: if he calls Lisa's bluff and she is not bluffing, he will lose all contact with his daughter; if she is bluffing and has no intention of surrendering the child, she can still retaliate by denying him access.

Of course, none of this is likely to cause any problems if you have a stable live-in relationship. You will raise your children together as married couples do, making decisions jointly on schooling, discipline, medical care and so on, and the fact that only the mother has legal rights will seldom, if ever, become an issue.

But a father – or potential father – should be aware that if his relationship with the mother of his illegitimate child ends unhappily and she decides to end all further contact between them, the law as it stands today offers him virtually no hope of seeing his child again.

WHAT ABOUT A PRIVATE CONTRACT?

Can a man and a woman who live together draw up a contract in which the woman agrees to share custody and guardianship of the child with her partner?

The answer, simply, is no. No attorney would ever draw up such an agreement and no court would enforce it, because the mother cannot surrender her parental rights and duties or any part of them to anyone else unless she gives the child up for adoption. In practice, of course, a stable live-in couple does share parental rights and duties. However, whenever there is a legal issue involved – for example, if consent is required for an operation, or if the child wants to marry before the age of 18, or if he or she has property or investments to administer – only the mother has the power to act on the child's behalf.

There is a remote possibility that the courts would uphold a private contract between the parents in which they agree that if they separate, the father will have the right to visit his child, as the mother would not be giving up any of her parental authority by agreeing to this. However, the court's ruling would be based on what it perceives to be in the best interests of the child.

If you do make such an agreement, it is a good idea to spell out clearly how often these visits will be allowed to take place, for example, every Sunday between 8 am and 8 pm, plus a two-week holiday once a year. This will prevent disputes from arising in the future over what constitutes 'reasonable' access. As with all other contracts, you should each keep a copy, signed by both of you, in a safe place.

WHOSE NAME WILL THE BABY HAVE?

A baby born outside marriage is normally registered in the name of the mother. However, it may be registered in the father's name if the father has acknowledged paternity in writing in the presence of the Registrar of Births and the mother has given her consent to the acknowledgement. The Registrar will not enter the name of any person as father unless both parents ask him to do so.

The registration of the birth of an extramarital child is governed by Section 10 of the Births, Marriages and Deaths Registration Act. Because of the ambiguous wording of this section, it is not clear whether the father's particulars may appear on the birth registration if the parents wish the child to have the mother's surname. Section 10 (3) states:

> The birth of the child born out of wedlock shall be registered under the surname of:
>
> (a) his mother; or
> (b) his father, provided the latter has made the acknowledgement contemplated in subsection (2) [i.e. acknowledged paternity] and the mother has consented.

This does not appear to say that the child *must* take the father's surname if the father's details appear in the birth register. Nor does it appear to say that the father's details must not appear if the child is registered in the mother's name. However, in the August 1990 edition of *Style* magazine a single mother related that when she and the father of her child asked to register the child in her name and yet state the father's particulars in the birth register, they were told that this was not allowed. When she insisted that the child have her surname, 'a great big red line and the word "unknown" [were] written across the section where the father's name should be.'

The Women's Legal Status Committee asked the Department of Home Affairs for clarification and here is the official reply from the office of the Director-General:

> As a rule the experience is that where the child's father acknowledges paternity the request is that the child be registered in his name, while if only the mother's par-

ticulars are available, the child is registered in her name. It does, however, appear to be plausible that the father gives full particulars, but that the request remains for registration in the mother's name.

As we saw in Paul's case above, the father does not acquire any parental rights by registering the child in his name.

The surname in an extramarital child's birth registration may be altered in certain circumstances. If the child was registered under the surname of his father but is known by the surname of his mother, the mother (or the child himself if he is over 21) may apply to have his birth registration amended. The new surname will then be inscribed in the birth register, but without erasing the previous surname. Conversely, an illegitimate child who was registered in his mother's name may apply to have his name in the birth register altered to that of his father. This will be allowed if his father acknowledges paternity in writing and his mother agrees to the change.

If the mother and father subsequently marry, they can apply to have the registration changed to read as if they had been married at the time the baby was born. The law allows this in order to protect as many children as possible from the label of illegitimacy: the child then becomes legitimate as from the time of his birth, no matter how many years after his birth the parents' marriage takes place.

IF THE PARENTS SUBSEQUENTLY MARRY

An illegitimate child becomes legitimate as soon as his mother and father marry. He then takes his father's surname and domicile, and the father acquires all the parental rights of a married father.

THE FATHER HAS A DUTY TO MAINTAIN HIS CHILD

The natural father is required by law to provide maintenance for his illegitimate child. This clearly poses no problem if he and the mother have a stable, loving relationship.

But difficulties can arise if the parents' relationship ends – particularly if it ends, as not infrequently happens, as a result of the pregnancy. No matter how publicly or how often the man has expressed his opposition to having children, however, he is still legally liable for maintenance if his partner, by accident or by design, falls pregnant and bears his child.

Conversely, the father who loves his child and wants to continue seeing the child after his relationship with the mother has ended cannot demand access as a *quid pro quo* for paying maintenance. As we saw above, he has a legal duty to provide financial support for his child, but no corresponding rights.

If the mother and father cannot agree on what constitutes reasonable maintenance, or if the father refuses to pay, the mother can apply to the maintenance officer at a magistrate's court for a maintenance order requiring him to provide financial support for the child. The court will then decide how much each of them should contribute to the child's upkeep, taking into consideration their respective means. Amendments to the Maintenance Act which will soon become law, will empower the court to make an order regarding responsibility for lying-in expenses and maintenance for the child from the date of birth, together with any interest due.

Failure to pay maintenance is a criminal offence and is dealt with accordingly. Unfortunately, many men cause their former partners severe financial hardship by habitually being late with maintenance payments, and many others escape their financial responsibilities entirely by simply disappearing.

If either parent dies while the child is still a minor, his or her estate becomes responsible for maintenance.

WHAT HAPPENS IF THE MAN NAMED AS FATHER CONTESTS PATERNITY?

If the man named by the woman as father of her extramarital child denies paternity, she will have to prove that the child is his before she can claim child maintenance from him. According to the law, the court will assume that a man who is proved to have had sex with the mother at a time when the child could have been conceived is the father. Presumably the fact that he was living with her at the time of conception would be regarded as proof that they had sexual relations; the court would then assume that he is the father unless he can provide convincing evidence that he is not (such as, for example, medical evidence that he has had a vasectomy or is impotent).

However, if paternity is still in doubt the court may order blood or tissue type tests to be done. These tests, which are done only when the baby is six months old, are conducted by the South African Institute for Medical Research and cost R543 for three people (mother, baby and one man). If two men could be the father of the baby, they will both be tested, at an additional cost per person of R181. This cost is usually, though not always, paid by the man. An amendment to the Maintenance Act which will soon become law provides that the state may pay for the tests if either the man or the woman is unable to pay.

The Institute checks three things: the blood grouping, hereditary enzymes, and the white cells or tissue in the blood. (Because they are called tissue type tests, many people believe that skin samples are taken as well as blood; this is not so, as the tissue referred to is contained in the blood.) The tests are exclusion tests: they can prove that the man is not the father, but can only indicate with varying degrees of probability that he could be. However, in some cases they can show a probability of up to 99,9%. If any person involved in a paternity suit refuses to allow the taking of blood samples, the court will presume that he or she is trying to conceal the truth, and draw its own conclusions.

THE MOTHER IS NOT ENTITLED TO MAINTENANCE

While the father is obliged to support his child, he is under no such obligation to pay maintenance to his former partner. Thus an unmarried mother is in a worse financial situation, if her relationship with the father of her child ends, than a married mother, who may be awarded maintenance by the court if she and her husband are divorced.

INHERITANCE

Both the mother and the father have the right to make a will leaving any part of their estate to their extramarital offspring.

If the mother dies without leaving a will (i.e. intestate), her illegitimate child or children will have the same right to inherit from her estate as any legitimate children she may have had.

Until recently, an illegitimate child was not entitled to inherit from his or her father if he died intestate. Nor could the father inherit from his intestate illegitimate child. However, this has now changed. The Intestate Succession Act No. 81 of 1987, which became law in March 1988, states that '... illegitimacy shall not affect the capacity of one blood relation to inherit the intestate estate of another blood relation.'

Therefore – assuming that the father has acknowledged paternity, or that the court has ruled that he is the father – both the father and the child may now inherit from the other's intestate estate. The intention of this Act was to place extramarital children on an equal footing with children born within marriage, and it is a welcome reform. As the Minister of Justice Mr H.J. Coetsee remarked in Parliament in 1987, '... fairness and justice ... require that a child should not be penalised for the sins of its parents.'

8

If you or your partner should die

None of us like to think about death – especially our own. Anyway, when we're young and fit, death seems very remote. Making a will and putting our financial affairs in order are things we always believe we'll have time to do 'tomorrow'.

Sadly, that is not always the case. South Africa has one of the worst accident fatality rates in the world, and young adults are more likely than anyone else to die on the road. No one is immune to fatal illness, even the most fanatically health-conscious.

It makes sense, therefore, to make a will and to take other steps to ensure that if you do die, your loved ones won't have a host of legal and financial problems to cope with in addition to their grief. This is good advice for anyone, but it is particularly important if you and your partner have a live-in relationship as opposed to a marriage.

In fact, Pat Clayton, author of *The Cohabitation Guidebook* (a handbook for live-in couples in England), comments wryly that 'Dying is one of the things you should try to avoid if you are cohabiting because unless you have done some careful planning all the various disadvantages of cohabiting come home to roost on the surviving partner.' After you've read the following story, which shows just how wrong things can go in the absence of 'careful planning', you'll probably agree with her.

MARC AND ANN: 'TOO MANY ASSUMPTIONS'

Marc is in his early 40s now, but with his longish hair, shaggy beard, jeans and bulky handknitted jersey he still looks like the hippie he was in the late sixties. That is when he first met Ann. They knew each other for three years before they decided to live together. Like many of their generation they believed that marriage robbed people of their independence and individuality, so they chose instead to say their own vows to each other on a beach near Cape Town one night. 'That was sufficient,' says Marc. 'We knew that our feelings were enduring and that we would stay together forever.'

Over the next eighteen years they led an extremely happy if unconventional life. Ann was a dress designer and at various times she owned a fashion boutique, had her own design studio and worked for a major clothing manufacturer. Marc also worked in the artistic field, sometimes doing graphic design, sometimes screenprinting, sometimes photography or magazine layouts. In addition, they almost always had a joint project on the go. For a number of years they had a flea market stall at which they sold T-shirts designed and sewn by Ann and silkscreened or handpainted by Marc. They also collaborated on commissions for wedding dresses.

At times they both had regular salaried jobs and money was plentiful; at other times, they both worked freelance and their monthly income fluctuated greatly. There were also long periods when either Marc or Ann was unemployed. They lost money on Ann's boutique as well as on a business venture of Marc's.

But they never argued over money, and cheerfully shared the bad times as well as the good. Marc says: 'When we moved in together we both had absolutely nothing. We always shared everything that we had – there was never any discussion about what belonged to whom. We both brought in what we could, and if it wasn't a good month it didn't matter. We were both happy. Ann was more disciplined about paying the monthly accounts, so I used to give her whatever I earned. Then if I needed money I'd ask her for some.' For years he didn't even have a bank account; Ann had a bank card that they both used when they wanted to draw money.

They were equally generous in their relationships with others. When Ann's mother lost her job they rented a bigger house and both the mother and her unemployed boyfriend came to live with them. Later, Ann's brother, newly divorced and also out of work, joined them. Marc and Ann supported all three until they found steady employment. For two years both Ann and Marc turned their pay-cheques over to the mother, who paid the accounts and ran the household. Several years later, when Ann's mother bought a house, they lived with her for three years and paid her rent. Even after they moved out, Ann continued to give money to her mother every month with Marc's knowledge and approval; Marc never asked, or cared, how much money she gave.

In 1981 Marc and Ann bought a small house in an older suburb of Johannesburg. Marc borrowed R5 000 from his employer for the deposit, which he paid into Ann's account. The house was regis-tered in Ann's name as Marc was in the process of starting a bus-iness and didn't want to put the house at risk. Five years later they sold the house for a profit of R50 000 and bought a second house in the same neighbourhood with the proceeds. It was also registered in Ann's name, and Marc signed surety for the bond.

Two years later, at the beginning of 1988, they were going through one of their periodic spells of financial difficulty. Ann, fed up with the fashion industry, had quit her job and was unemployed for three months. Marc's business was in trouble and his partners had pulled out. He was on the verge of closing the company down when Ann suggested that she come and work with him and help him to save the business. She got a personal loan of R25 000 from the bank to pay off the company's debts and moved into one of the offices vacated by Marc's former partners.

A few weeks later Ann woke up feeling ill. At first they didn't worry about it, but when she was still feeling dreadful four days later she went to see their doctor. After a perfunctory examination he told her it was a particularly nasty strain of flu. She went back home but her condition worsened steadily over the next few days. By the time she finally went to hospital, where her illness was cor-rectly diagnosed as tick bite fever, it was too late. She lapsed into a *coma, and two weeks after becoming ill she died. She had just turned 40.*

Marc was devastated – and totally unprepared for the second blow which came several weeks later. Ann's mother phoned to tell him that she had sought legal advice regarding Ann's estate. The lawyer had told her that, as Marc and Ann had never married and Ann had died intestate (i.e. without leaving a will), Ann's entire estate belonged to her and Ann's brother and sister. Marc was entitled to nothing.

Shocked and disbelieving, Marc also went to see a lawyer, who confirmed what Ann's mother had told him. However, the lawyer believed that Marc had grounds for claiming half of the estate on the basis that he and Ann had had an implied 'universal partnership'. Marc retained him to prepare a case.

In the meantime Marc continued to live in the house and pay the bond. He also kept up payments on the R25 000 personal loan that Ann had taken out just before her death. Medical aid covered R18 000 of Ann's medical bills but Marc paid the balance of R6 000 out of his own pocket. A few months after Ann's death he had to give up his office in town to pay his rapidly mounting legal fees.

Over two and a half years later the case was finally heard in the Supreme Court. After the first day of testimony the judge stated that the matter should never have come before the court. He advised both advocates to urge their clients to settle privately. Marc's lawyers had sought an out-of-court settlement for over two years but had always been rebuffed by Ann's family. Finally, on the fourth day of the trial, Ann's family instructed their advocate to settle.

The agreement eventually reached was that Marc would pay Ann's family R45 000 and accept liability for half of Ann's loan. In return, he would get the house and most of the furniture. Marc's legal bills are still coming in; to date they exceed R50 000. It is probably a fair assumption that Ann's family has paid a similar amount.

Marc is now a great deal poorer but wiser. He comments: 'We assumed we were living in a common-law marriage and conducted

our lives as if we were living in community of property. I also
never thought Ann's family would do anything like this. As far as
I was concerned we were one big extended family – Ann's mother
was like my own mum. I know Ann wouldn't have expected it
either. I can see now that there were just too many assumptions on
our part.'

Marc and Ann had a warm, loving, unselfish relationship, one
that puts many marriages to shame. 'In our eyes we were more
"married" than any of our friends – than any of her family, for that
matter,' he says.

True ... but "married" is not the same as married. If you and
your partner have never married, you are single – there is no
such thing in South Africa as a common-law marriage. Living
together without taking that into account is a sure-fire recipe
for added grief if one of you dies.

INTESTATE SUCCESSION

If Ann and Marc had been married and she had died intestate,
Marc, as surviving spouse, would have inherited her entire
estate according to the Intestate Succession Act.

The estate of any person who dies without leaving a will is
settled according to this Act, which sets out very clearly who
will succeed, in what order and in what proportions.

If the deceased is survived by a spouse but not by a child, the
spouse will inherit the entire estate. If the deceased is survived
by a child but not by a spouse, the child will inherit the entire
estate (this now includes illegitimate children).

The Act goes on to stipulate how the estate will be divided if
the deceased leaves both a spouse and a child (or children), if
he leaves neither spouse nor children but parents, and so on
down the line of blood relations from nearest to furthest. If the
deceased is not survived by a spouse or any blood relations
whatsoever, the estate will be forfeited to the state.

Live-in partners, as Marc discovered, don't even get a look-
in. They are entitled to nothing under the terms of the Act.

Only family members can inherit, even if the deceased has been estranged from his or her family for fifty years.

IF ANN HAD MADE A WILL

If Ann had left a will, her estate would have been settled according to her wishes. She could have made Marc sole beneficiary or divided her estate between him and the members of her family in whatever way she chose.

UNIVERSAL PARTNERSHIP

As stated above, Marc's lawyers prepared his case on the grounds that he and Ann had had a universal partnership and that he was therefore entitled to half her estate when she died. The problem was that Marc and Ann had never expressly entered into a partnership agreement, either orally or in writing; they had simply shared everything without ever discussing the matter. Marc's lawyers therefore had to prove that universal partnership in their case was implied by their conduct.

A universal partnership is one of the oldest forms of partnership and was very popular in the Middle Ages, particularly among members of a family or a craft guild. Today, however, it is extremely rare. The parties to a universal partnership agree to put in common all their property both present and future. 'Everything is included in this partnership which comes to each of the partners under any title whatever, even by succession, gift or legacy ... except what comes to one of the partners on condition that it will not fall into the partnership' (*Partnership*, J.J. Henning and H.J. Delport, Butterworth, 1984). Because of its all-inclusive nature it is not suitable for most commercial ventures. According to one legal authority a universal partnership most closely resembles a benefit society established for the advantage of its members.

As with any other type of partnership, a universal partnership must satisfy four legal requirements. These are 1) that the aim of the partnership must be to make a profit; 2) that both parties must contribute to the enterprise; 3) that the partnership must operate for the benefit of both parties; and 4)

92

that the contract between the two parties must be legitimate.

The contract does not have to be written to be legitimate: it may be tacit or implied (as Marc's lawyers argued it was with him and Ann). In a case involving universal partnership in 1945 the judge held that 'If the agreement is not in writing the intention of the parties must be ascertained from their words and conduct.' Similarly, the judge in a 1984 case ruled that 'the principle is firmly established that any contract can be brought about by conduct.'

The 1984 case involved a couple who had been married according to Islamic law, and this raises an important point: a man and a woman who are married only in a religious ceremony by a person who is not an officially authorised marriage officer are in the same legal position as a live-in couple who have never married (except for income tax purposes). They will not be protected by marriage law unless they are also married by a recognised marriage officer such as a magistrate.

THE WORST POSSIBLE OUTCOME

It seems likely that the judge would have ruled in Marc's favour if the trial had continued. But that is not the point. The point is that for Marc to have to rely on the ability of a team of expensive lawyers to prove the existence of an implied universal partnership was the worst possible ending to a long and loving relationship.

If he and Ann had been married, or if Ann had left a will, a trial would have been completely unnecessary. Her partner of eighteen years would have been spared two and a half years of emotional stress and over R50 000 in legal fees.

It needn't have happened to Marc. It needn't happen to you either. All you have to do is make a will.

MAKING A WILL

A lot of people are under the impression that making a will is an expensive business. It isn't. Unless your affairs are very complicated a lawyer will charge you about R250 to R300 to draw up a will. When you weigh that against the legal expenses your survivors could face if you die intestate, it is clearly a good investment. Alternatively, your bank can help you make a will. Usually it will not charge you for this service as long as you name the bank as executor of your estate. However, one major bank now levies an administration fee of R150 if the estate exceeds R200 000 in value.

Of course, there is nothing to stop you from making your own will without expert advice. However, unless you are very knowledgeable about the law, it just isn't worth it. If your wording is at all ambiguous, for example, your home-made will could cause as many headaches and expenses for your survivors as no will at all.

You may believe you don't have enough assets to justify the trouble and expense of making a will. But chances are that you are wrong. You can easily test this by making a list of your possessions. Even if you don't own a house, you probably have at least some of the following: a car, furniture, appliances, a television set, a video recorder, a stereo system, jewellery, records, tapes and books. If you make a rough estimate of the value of these you will find that your estate is not as insignificant as you thought. Monetary value aside, you may want your partner to have your car and your brother to have your stereo if you die. You can ensure this only by leaving a will.

If you own the house in which you and your partner are living and want him or her to inherit it if you die, a will is essential. The same is true if you and your partner own a house jointly and you want your half-share to go to your partner if you die.

The law permits you, with certain limitations, to leave your property to anyone. You can even disinherit your children if you wish, though minor children are legally entitled to maintenance from your estate.

If you decide to alter anything in your will at a later stage, either because your circumstances have changed or because you have changed your mind about how you want to distribute your assets, you can revise your existing will or revoke it entirely and make a new one. But you cannot revise your existing will merely by pencilling in the changes and additions. These all have to be properly witnessed and signed. An important thing to note here is that, according to the formalities laid down by the Wills Act, no person who is named as a beneficiary in your will may sign the will as a witness.

If you are the mother of an illegitimate child, you can appoint a guardian for your child in your will. According to the law, the father of an illegitimate child has no rights in regard to the child; if you want him to become the child's guardian if you die, you must include a clause to that effect in your will.

IF DEATH IS CAUSED BY THE WRONGFUL ACT OF A THIRD PARTY

Doris and Ed, both in their late 40s, had been living together for twelve years. Doris hadn't worked for the past ten years because Ed's job required that he travel a lot and he liked her to accompany him. Then one day when Ed was alone in the car, the driver of another car went through a red light and hit Ed's car broadside. Ed was killed instantly.

If Doris and Ed had been married, Doris would have been entitled to sue the driver for damages for the loss of support she sustained as a result of Ed's death. However, as Doris discovered, live-in partners do not have this right. The reason is that while husbands and wives have a legal duty to support one another, live-in partners do not. Therefore, Doris could not claim damages from the guilty person because she was never legally entitled to the financial support she lost as a result of Ed's death.

If Doris and Ed had had a child, the child would have had the right to claim damages because a child is legally entitled to be supported by both its parents. This applies to illegitimate children as well as to children born in marriage.

WORKMEN'S COMPENSATION

If your partner dies as a result of injuries he received during the course of his work, you may be able to claim compensation.

The Workmen's Compensation Act is one of the few pieces of legislation that extends rights to a live-in partner, provided that she was 'at the time of the accident ... wholly or partly dependent on the workman for the necessaries of life'. However, if your partner was still legally married to another woman at the time of his death, her claim will take precedence.

The Act applies to almost all workmen who earn less than R36 000 a year. (There are some exceptions, for example the self-employed, domestic workers and members of the Defence Force who are killed in the line of duty.) This figure is adjusted from time to time for inflation.

When you make a claim you will be required to sign a statement to the effect that 'neither the workman nor I was legally married, but we were living together as man and wife'. The Commissioner in charge of processing the claim may then ask for affidavits from your church, friends or colleagues as proof of this.

If you and your partner had children together, the children are entitled to claim compensation. The fact that they are illegitimate does not affect their right to do so.

INSURANCE

Insurance offers another way for you and your partner to provide financial security for each other in the event that one of you dies. For example, you can each take out a policy on your own life and either name your partner as beneficiary or cede the policy to him or her.

Alternatively, you may insure your partner's life if you have an 'insurable interest' in him or her – in other words, if you stand to lose financially if he or she dies. The amount of cover you are allowed to take out is determined by the amount you stand to lose in the event of your partner's death. You are deemed to have an insurable interest in your partner if you are registered as joint owners of a house, for example.

Banks and building societies strongly encourage home-buyers to take out life cover for the total value of the bond. In some cases, they may refuse to grant a bond unless a life assurance policy is pledged to them as collateral while the mortgage is outstanding.

PENSIONS

If your partner belongs to a pension fund you may be entitled to all, or a portion of, the benefits payable if he or she dies. However, this is not certain, and depends on a number of rather complicated factors.

According to the law governing pension funds, which was revised in mid-1989, pension benefits may be paid either to the dependants of the deceased pension fund member or to a nominee, or to both dependants and nominee in any proportion the trustee of the fund judges to be fair.

The Act's definition of dependants includes both *legal* dependants and *factual* dependants of the fund member – in other words, those people the member was *legally* liable to maintain (such as a spouse and children) and those people whom the member was *in fact* maintaining, even though he was not legally obliged to do so. As a live-in partner you are not a legal dependant, but the trustee of the fund may find that you are a factual dependant. If you are financially independent of your partner, of course, you will not qualify as his or her factual dependant.

The member can designate any person as his or her nominee, but must do so in writing to the fund. The member can state whether he or she wishes the nominee to receive the entire benefit or a specified portion of it. The trustee of the fund will take the member's wishes into consideration, but as dependants have first claim, the trustee may award less to the nominee than the member stipulated.

It is important to note that if your partner designated you as his or her nominee prior to June 1989, this designation is no longer valid and must be made anew.

9

Cohabitation contracts

To many couples who live together, the greatest advantage their relationship offers is freedom from all the legal duties and obligations, regulations, restrictions and paperwork that go hand in hand with marriage. So why, then, are we beginning to hear a lot of talk about the need for cohabitation contracts?

The reason is simply this: more and more people are realising that freedom from regulation has a price. It is all a matter of costs and benefits. A married person has the benefit of legal rights, for which the price is legal obligations. In a live-in relationship, costs and benefits are reversed: the benefit is no legal obligations, but the cost is no legal rights.

Living together in South Africa today is a lot like playing a sport in which there are no rules: it may be fun initially, but if play becomes rough, someone is likely to get hurt. And when that happens, there is no point in crying 'foul', because if there are no rules, anything goes. In the words of Professor Frieda Francisco-La Grange of the Department of Social Work at RAU, 'the personal freedom so attractive at the beginning [of a live-in relationship] spells legal abandonment at the end.'

The obvious way to overcome the problem of legal abandonment is to establish your *own* rules at the start of your relationship. You can do this with a cohabitation contract, which is a written agreement between you and your partner clarifying your financial arrangements and stating what will happen if your relationship ends. Cohabitation contracts are now common in a number of countries overseas. For example, live-in couples in the Canadian province of Ontario were encouraged by the Family Law Reform Act of 1978 to enter into a written agreement. They are still fairly rare in South Africa, but several prominent legal experts here strongly recommend them for live-in couples.

Emotional objections

Some people – usually women – are horrified by the whole idea of cohabitation contracts. It all sounds so cold and mercenary, they object: contracts are for impersonal business partnerships, not love relationships. But think about it for a moment: if you and your partner remain together for a number of years, buy furniture and perhaps a house together, your financial commitment to your relationship may be as great as – or even greater than – any business investment you are likely to make. That doesn't mean you have to be cold and calculating, but it is certainly a good reason to be practical and prudent.

When your future financial security could be at risk, it is foolhardy to rely on oral promises and agreements, no matter how sincerely they may have been made at the time. Remember the words of the late great Hollywood movie mogul Sam Goldwyn: 'A verbal contract isn't worth the paper it's written on.'

WHAT TO INCLUDE IN A COHABITATION CONTRACT

In general, the most important matters to consider in a contract are: 1) how expenses are to be divided; 2) how property and assets are to be owned (i.e. jointly or separately or a combination of the two); and 3) how joint assets are to be divided if the relationship ends.

The way in which you and your partner choose to handle these matters depends on your own circumstances and preferences. If you both work and your salaries are more or less the same, you may decide to contribute equally to expenses. If one

99

of you earns more than the other, you may choose to share expenses pro rata. You may decide to buy all movable assets separately; alternatively, you may elect to buy them jointly, though if that is the case your agreement should set out clearly how they will be divided if your relationship ends. If your partner works while you stay at home to look after small children, you may agree that he will pay for all expenses but that any assets you acquire will be shared equally if you part.

If your partner owns the house you live in, you may agree in the contract that, if your relationship ends, he or she will compensate you for any home improvements (landscaping, built-in cupboards etc) that you have financed. It is better, though, to agree that all home improvements will be the financial responsibility of the partner who owns the house. If you own the house jointly, there are a number of important issues that should be covered in a cohabitation contract. (These are discussed in Chapter 6.) If you and your partner rent accommodation, you may want to include matters such as liability for rent and security of tenure.

An important issue for some women who don't have an income – either because they are looking after children or because their partners like them to stay at home – is that of maintenance. A husband is legally obliged to support his wife, and though the courts are moving away from the notion that every woman is entitled to lifelong support after divorce, they may award maintenance to those former wives who clearly need it.

A woman who lives with her partner, on the other hand, is not entitled to support. If her partner walks out or evicts her, she may suddenly find herself homeless and destitute, with no marketable skills with which to earn a living. If this could happen to you, it is reasonable to ask your partner for an agreement that if your relationship ends he will pay you rehabilitative maintenance for a specified period to give you time to acquire the means to support yourself.

If you have children, the law does not permit you to agree to share custody or guardianship. However, an agreement that

100

the father will have reasonable access to the children if your relationship breaks up may be accepted by the courts.

GET LEGAL ADVICE

When it comes to drawing up a contract, it makes sense to get expert advice. An attorney can explain all the options that are available to you and advise you on which one is best suited to your situation. For example, a cohabitation contract may in some circumstances be drawn up as a universal partnership agreement. Alternatively, it may be modelled on the antenuptial contract based on the accrual system.

Moreover, if you want your contract to be legally enforceable, it must satisfy a number of legal requirements, and it is unlikely that a home-made contract will do so. A few hundred rands in lawyers' fees now could end up saving you a great deal more in the long run.

WILL THE COURTS ENFORCE COHABITATION CONTRACTS?

There is, ironically, still a slight possibility that the courts will refuse to enforce *any* cohabitation contract, no matter how expertly it has been drawn up. The reason is that, according to the law of contract, a contract is unenforceable if it is contrary to good morals. This includes any contract to reward extramarital sex.

Until about 1970 there was virtually unanimous agreement among legal experts in South Africa, America and most Commonwealth countries that a contract between unmarried partners was based on, and inseparable from, their immoral sexual relationship. In other words, it was a contract to reward extramarital sex, and therefore illegal.

After 1970, however, as living together became more and more prevalent overseas, that line of reasoning came under vigorous attack. Critics argued that it was out of step with public attitudes, as most people no longer regarded live-in relationships as immoral. In the words of an American judge: 'The mores of society have indeed changed so radically in

101

regard to cohabitation that we cannot impose a standard based on alleged moral considerations that have apparently been so widely abandoned by so many.'

As a result, most American courts have done an about-face and now rule that a contract between live-in partners concerning their expenses and property rights is enforceable as long as sex is not part of the consideration for the agreement. If a couple states in their contract that they are lovers or that the contract will terminate if they cease to be lovers, the courts would probably refuse to enforce it. But a straightforward financial agreement would be enforced by most American courts. The late Professor H.R. Hahlo wrote in 1985, 'It is submitted that this is also the law in South Africa.'

The overseas debate for and against enforcement of cohabitation contracts has been followed with great interest by the legal profession here and will influence the deliberations of our courts when they are asked to make a ruling. Ultimately, however, their decision will be based on local precedents and what they believe is appropriate to South African attitudes and conditions.

In this regard there is an intriguing case in the South African Law Reports about a couple who lived together for 21 years, had two children and ran a painting and decorating contracting business together until his death. The man was legally married to another woman throughout the period of this relationship. He and his live-in partner never entered into a written agreement about their financial affairs. Nevertheless, the court ruled that there had been an *implied* universal partnership agreement between the man and his live-in partner. Accordingly, it awarded her half of his deceased estate.

The reason this case is so intriguing is that it was heard in 1953 in the Orange Free State. If a Free State court in those unenlightened times was willing to recognise an implied partnership contract between live-in partners, one of whom was committing adultery, it certainly seems likely that our courts today will uphold an express cohabitation contract entered into by two unmarried adults.

102

10

The myth and the reality

There's a saying attributed to Mark Twain that goes: 'The trouble with people isn't what they don't know. It's what they know that ain't so.' There is a lot of truth in that. One of the greatest causes of hardship for people involved in live-in relationships in this country is their belief that they are married in common law and therefore have quasi-marital rights. As this book has repeatedly stressed, it just ain't so. It is time we put the myth of the common-law marriage to rest before it does any more harm.

It doesn't matter how many years you live together or how much you love each other: the law regards you and your partner as two single people who happen to have the same address. That is the reality, and you are courting disaster if you fail to take it into account.

Marc, who spent over R50 000 in a two-year legal battle because his partner died without making a will (see Chapter 8), said when he finished relating his story: 'If reading about my experience persuades just one couple to sit down and sort out their affairs, I'll feel that it wasn't all entirely in vain.'

Appendix

In the 1985 Census 3% of the total population classified them-selves as 'living together'. The percentage was highest for col-oureds (3,7%) and lowest for Asians (0,9%), with whites and blacks in between at 1,2% and 3,5% respectively.

However, it is more significant to look at the percentage of people within a given age group who are living together. Taking the 20 to 34-year age group as an example, 5,8% of all South Africans aged 20 to 34 were living together in 1985. Broken down into population groups, the percentages are: coloureds, 7,3%; blacks, 6,6%; whites, 2,8%; and Asians, 1,8%.

In all population groups, living together was most common in the 20 to 29-year age group (ranging as a percentage from 33% of all black cohabitants to 42% of all white cohabitants), and second most common among people aged 30 to 39.

Unfortunately the Census did not give a further breakdown of these figures to show the economic status, education levels or religions of the people involved in live-in relationships, nor did it enumerate the number of children living with parents who were not married to each other.

The figures below give the numbers of people living to-gether in 1985 according to age and population group, rounded off to the nearest hundred.

Whites:	1 700 under age 20
	22 700 age 20–29
	14 500 age 30–39
	8 300 age 40–49
	7 000 over age 50

Coloureds:	4 400 under age 20
	38 600 age 20–29
	29 300 age 30–39
	17 400 age 40–49
	13 800 over age 50

Asians:	500 under age 20
	2 800 age 20–29
	2 100 age 30–39
	1 200 age 40–49
	1 300 over age 50

Blacks:	16 200 under age 20
	175 300 age 20–29
	156 500 age 30–39
	97 953 age 40–49
	87 700 over age 50

Index